CW01023127

KEEPING UP WITH TEACHING

KEEPING UP

UP

STRATEGIES FOR THRIVING
IN THE 21ST CENTURY

WITH
TEACHING

CELIA DI IORIO
MARGHERITA GHEZZI

amba
press

Published in 2024 by Amba Press, Melbourne, Australia
www.ambapress.com.au

© Celia Di Iorio and Margherita Ghezzi 2024

All rights reserved. No part of this book may be reproduced or transmitted in
any form or by any means, electronic or mechanical, including photocopying,
recording or by any information storage and retrieval system, without prior
permission in writing from the publisher.

Cover design: Tess McCabe
Internal design: Amba Press
Editor: Brooke Lyons

ISBN: 9781923215122 (pbk)
ISBN: 9781923215139 (ebk)

A catalogue record for this book is available from the National Library of Australia.

Contents

Acknowledgements

To our families, Rohan, Lily, Angelo, Jason, Lexi, Mavi and Maurizio. Thank you for your never-ending love.

To our furry family members, Maui and Elvis. Thank you for creating a sense of calm and reassurance.

To Professor Susanne Garvis and Associate Professor Wendy Goff, a heartfelt thank you: your guidance and support has been invaluable to us.

To Emma-Kate Comito: thank you for your insights as a graduate teacher, we wish you every success as you keep up with teaching.

To our fellow colleagues, in particular Luc, Ebony, Michael, Rhonni, David and Louise. Thank you for your continuous support and insightful contributions to our book and for the positive impact you make to our profession.

To Amba Press. Thank you for giving us the opportunity and confidence to get our words and thoughts out into the world.

A note from the authors

Dear graduate teachers,

You've got this! How do we know? Because we were once graduates ourselves, and have survived and thrived as teachers in the 21st century. Marghi graduated in 2005 as an international student and went on to work as a secondary teacher and later in the publishing, curriculum development and higher education sectors. Celia graduated in 1999 and went on to work as a primary school teacher and wellbeing leader, later joining Marghi in the higher education sector. This is where we first met.

We became great buddies, connecting through our shared passion for teaching and learning, and supporting pre-service and early graduate teachers. We spent many hours over the years discussing our own experiences in teaching, the challenges our teaching profession faced and the adaptability and resilience teachers need to thrive. Teacher wellbeing underpinned all our discussions, along with the importance of developing a healthy balance between personal and professional identity.

From as young as we can remember, teaching was our dream, and it's who we are at heart today. Teaching is a unique profession where moments of chaos are followed by clarity and vice versa. The emotions you will feel are real, from the triumphant highs of a student succeeding to the challenging lows of things not working as planned. But through it all, there is one thing that remains consistent:

a teacher's ability to make a difference, one lesson at a time. You can do this not just for your students, but for yourself as well.

If we could turn back time there are a few things we would tell our graduate selves. So, from us to you, here are the most important things to keep in mind:

- Be kind to yourself, and remember that learning is a cycle of adapting and growing.
- Develop reflective practices. Ask yourself, what went well? What could I do differently next time? These simple questions can help you remember your successes, which we often forget.
- Set goals you can achieve and boundaries you can maintain. For example, when you have finished writing five report cards, take some time to do something for yourself.
- Ask for help. If you don't know, ask. Spend time making connections with your colleagues and find someone you trust who will answer your questions.
- Remember that you won't always see the impact you are having immediately. But one day you will receive a card, a note or an acknowledgement from a student that will make you smile far beyond the end of your career.
- Finally, don't worry. With time, things became easier. The initial panic dissipates and the stuff that you stressed about becomes second nature.

Remember, you won't always be a graduate. One day you will be an experienced teacher. Remember the lessons you are learning and the opportunities you're experiencing so that you too can pay it forward.

We wish you every success.

Celia and Marghi

Introduction

One of the most rewarding aspects of being a teacher is the important role you will play in the community. Teachers are role models and influencers who can help transform and shape a student's life. As Loris Malaguzzi said, 'We need to redefine the role of the teacher as one who is constantly learning along with the children, as opposed to simply imparting knowledge upon them.' With this in mind, we must remember how our emotions impact our thoughts and relationships not only with others, but with ourselves.

In the Australian context, we are fortunate to teach in a country that is rich in remarkable multicultural influences, which enrich much of what is taught and how. This can help positively motivate us on our teaching journey and provide reminders that our actions have consequences, and our words have great power.

While recognising that teaching is, indeed, a strongly compliance-based profession, this book aims to redirect attention to your mental and emotional wellbeing as a graduate teacher. We consider you as a whole person, focusing on the bigger picture to support health and happiness. This will ultimately support you in building positive relationships with students, parents and colleagues, which contributes to everyone's wellbeing in a school community.

Each chapter focuses on a key wellbeing standard from the official Teacher Subjective Wellbeing Questionnaire – an eight-item self-report rating scale for measuring teachers' job-specific wellbeing

(Renshaw, 2022; Renshaw et al., 2015). It comprises two subscales: school connectedness, and teaching efficacy. Scores can be used as standalone wellbeing indicators or summed to create an overall teacher subjective wellbeing composite score. This survey is recommended by the Australian Institute for Teaching and School Leadership (AITSL) to 'scale' educators' wellbeing for research.

At the start of each chapter, you will find words from influential masters who have shaped education. As you read through the chapters, keep these words at the forefront of your mind, allowing them to inspire you to never give up and keep working on being the teacher you want to be.

Each chapter also begins with a story outlining an individual educator's lived experience. We will use these experiences to help you identify key learnings and draw possible solutions and strategies for survival and progress.

Each chapter ends with some final words. This is where connections between the influential master quotations at the beginning and the content throughout meet, leaving you with food for thought.

Let's dive in and get started! Time to reflect and make things happen.

CHAPTER 1

I FEEL LIKE I BELONG AT THIS SCHOOL

Through others, we become ourselves.

– Lev Vygotsky

Marghi's story

I spent the last few months of my initial teacher education (ITE) degree stressing about my English as an additional language or dialect (EAL/D) background. Here I was, an experienced teacher from Italy, retraining to become a teacher in Australia, and the only thing I could focus on was my accent. I hated being asked about it.

I remember that all my ITE peers back then were stressing about something. There were other pre-service teachers who had different cultural backgrounds like me, but I could only see the worse in me. My stress turned into fretting. Would I belong? Would I be able to conform to the idea of what others thought a great educator sounded like?

No matter how much we learnt about equity and diversity, somehow I could not shake that feeling of not belonging. Would anyone ever want me as a teacher? Would students accept me? Would parents accept me? Would my peers accept me? I was ultimately, in my own self-assessment, placing myself in the category of not being good enough to belong to the profession of teaching in the Australian context. The fact that I had years of teaching experience on the other side of the world, had received positive and encouraging feedback from my mentor teachers during placements, and had successfully completed the IELTS English test, anxiety precluded me from thinking clearly.

After all the stressing and fretting I graduated and began the process of applying for teaching positions. To my utter surprise, I received a call offering me a position as an EAL/D, Humanities and Language teacher at a school in Springvale, Melbourne. To this day, I still remember thinking how desperate the school must have been to hire me.

I spent the lead-up to my start date thinking about how to better myself and be the best version of myself. At least, that's what I made myself believe. Really, I was thinking about how to hide who I was and be what I thought the school wanted me to be.

Then my first day of teaching in Australia arrived. I stood at the door of my classroom welcoming each student in my best Italian accent, and it was at that point that I realised not only did I have an accent, but so did two-thirds of the students and parents who were walking through my door.

Slowly I started letting go of the feeling of having to hide or change who I was. Instead I started focusing on how who I was could support my students' learning journeys. With this, my sense of belonging grew. It was not always easy to manage students in a highly multicultural context, and many graduates before me had left; but I knew I belonged there.

Building your story

It can be challenging to find the time to reflect on yourself and your practice. Taking the time to reflect is an effective form of professional learning. It helps to consider your journey and evaluate what has been successful, and any changes that need to be made. It is important to learn from practice and to be part of a culture that values continuous improvement. Stephen Brookfield (Brookfield, 2010) offers four perspectives that can assist you to reflect as a teaching professional from different vantage points: autobiographical, learner, colleague and literature.

For now, focus on the autobiographical. How does your own background and experiences impact your practice? Think about the image you hold of yourself in relation to entering a school setting for the first time. What language would you use to describe yourself? Is it deficit or strength-based? What are your self-limiting beliefs? What could you do to reframe your perspective to overcome any biases you have about yourself?

What experienced teachers say

Self-limiting biases may be influencing your ability to reach personal and professional goals and your sense of belonging. When you analyse these biases in a thoughtful way, your brain may say, 'That is ridiculous! Why am I following that rule?'. Due to past experiences, challenges or false interpretations, these biases are hidden in the heart of our being and have perhaps never been consciously evaluated nor seen through an objective lens.

If you are having trouble making connections in a new school, we encourage you to consider whether you have been unconsciously living by any secret rules you have set yourself. You are not alone. Remember: all teachers were once graduates, and all have stories that helped shape them today. We asked some experienced teachers to think back on the self-limiting beliefs they had in their early teaching days. Maybe you can relate to some of these experiences.

> My mantra was, 'Only difficult goals count.' I felt guilty if something came naturally or I was having fun while teaching. I used to think that if I was not stressed all the time when going to school as a graduate, I must not have been working hard enough or not being productive. Over time I have learnt to appreciate the small wins and understand how important they are to developing your teaching practice. – *Jodie*

> 'I'm just not qualified to do this.' This was my biggest bias when I got my first teaching gig. Whether it was implementing new strategies, taking a greater role in the classroom or investing in an extracurricular activity, I used to get bogged down thinking about my shortcomings or perceived inadequacies and end up missing out on tremendous opportunities to make a difference. – *Jackson*

*I had this preconceived idea that 'I need to do this all on my own.' This led me to believe that getting help was a sign of weakness. Perfectionism can be very isolating, but it was my way of avoiding failure and judgement. My teaching partner noticed that I was not spending time in the staffroom and was leaving work significantly later than most. We had a chat and I realised that I needed to make changes to challenge my existing mindset. I started to seek more opportunities to collaborate with colleagues, especially with challenges that had me stumped. Through this process, I found that I too was able to support my colleagues, and my sense of belonging started to develop. You must learn to find a healthy balance between independent work and collaboration. – **Loue***

What is belonging?

Within a school community, belonging refers to students' and teachers' feelings of being accepted and valued by peers and by others at the school. It reflects the extent to which students and teachers feel personally accepted, respected, included and supported (NSW Department of Education, n.d.).

Belonging has a strong influence on motivation and outcomes, and is linked to a teacher's professional and academic achievements. Belonging is also linked to happiness. Those who have a strong sense of belonging tend to be happier, have greater interest in school responsibilities and feel more confident within themselves. When teachers do not feel they belong at school they tend to reject school values and withdraw from school responsibilities, which can lead them to alienate themselves (Lemon, 2022).

AITSL's Australian Professional Standards for Teachers help teachers understand and develop their practice and expertise to have maximum impact on all learners (AITSL, n.d.). Belonging underpins Professional Standard 7, which requires us to engage in professional learning with colleagues, parents/carers and the community. Belonging also underpins all other standards by allowing for professional knowledge and practice to develop.

Passing your sense of belonging on

Belonging supports school connection, allowing you to build relationships between yourself, colleagues, students, parents and the local community.

You and your school

A school is an ecosystem, defined by the *Oxford English Dictionary* as 'a biological community of interacting organisms and their physical environment'. This has tremendous implications for how we conduct ourselves within them.

You may not be teaching in another country where they speak a language different to your native tongue; but entering a new school community means entering a whole new ecological system. Each school has its own history, values and socio-cultural context, as well as its own micro cosmos represented by the interactions between multiple people from diverse backgrounds.

Bronfenbrenner's (1979) ecological systems theory holds that we encounter different environments throughout our lifespan that may influence our behaviour to varying degrees. This theory can help us understand why we may behave differently when we are in the presence of our family or when we are at work, and it also helps us understand why this happens to others that we meet at school. Upon entering a school, you are adding a new identity to that system. It is key to appreciate and respect the school as an established context and consider how you may impact it. Developing intercultural awareness is key as a teaching professional (Steele and Leming, 2022).

Think of your first teaching gig as if you are travelling to a new place and learning about its culture, its people and the dos and don'ts. This will shift your perspective and make the journey more enjoyable. Every element of a school affects other parts, including yourself. If you believe that a school is an ecosystem, you realise you must care about every aspect of the school, including yourself.

 Think about all the interactions and interdependencies within a school and how they affect the ecosystem. For example, how is cultural diversity supported within the school?

You and your students

As a teacher you are a critical influencer who can impact a student's learning in a positive or negative way. Students can sense a teacher's feelings. One of the ways you can support your students in developing a sense of belonging is by example. Through developing healthy connections yourself, as the teacher within the school community, you can enable your students to understand how to belong. When you feel connected, you are happier and less anxious, and this transfers to students.

There is growing research evidence that strong teacher–student relationships can promote school belonging, even though creating these relationships within highly complex educational systems can be challenging. There is a correlation between a teacher's sense of belonging and that of their students, so the effort is totally worth it in the long run (Allen et al., 2021).

In 2019, researchers from UNSW Sydney surveyed 2079 students in 18 high schools across Australia, and again 12 months later (UNSW, 2019). Professor Andrew Martin and Dr Rebecca Collie assessed the quality of students' relationships with teachers and students' academic engagement, including class participation and enjoyment of school. They found that, 'Every additional positive relationship with a teacher was associated with greater engagement. That is, students participated more in class, they had more enjoyment in their learning, and their aspirations grew.' Importantly, when they compared the effects of positive and negative teacher–student relationships, they found that the benefits of positive relationships outweighed the negative effects of poor relationships. In other words, positive teacher–student relationships impacted students' engagement more.

To enhance your students' sense of belonging it is important to provide emotional support when needed, and adjust your teaching to meet diverse needs. Remember to also adjust your personal expectations along the way. It takes experience and many cycles of growth to master your relationships with students. Engage in a process of ongoing reflection to help build your teacher identity.

 Think of a time a teacher's influence impacted your learning.

You and your colleagues

As a pre-service or graduate teacher, your connection with your mentor teacher, teaching partner, teaching team and wider teaching community directly impacts your sense of belonging. If you are connected to your colleagues, you can work more effectively with each other (Lemon et al., 2022).

A practical strategy to increase your sense of belonging to a school is to actively engage in opportunities for connection such as communities of practice, coaching opportunities and networking with peers. This can start with informal catch-ups in the staffroom or before or after school. It is critical that you engage in sharing stories, lived experiences and reflections, and create professional spaces for growth with your colleagues. Beyond what you learn during placement and through university, you should also discuss your ideas around career longevity, gender roles, work-life balance, institutional challenges, the sense of self and identity with your colleagues. These conversations provide opportunities to create precious learning moments. Sharing lived experiences helps you develop self-awareness and resilience and sparks ideas, which ultimately supports you to cultivate your teaching identity and sense of belonging. You will understand yourself as an educator better through other educators. Engaging in these professional conversations means you're contributing to creating and expanding safe spaces for others to share their professional and personal stories. You can connect with others through your challenges, and acquire strategies to navigate early teaching and understand the school's core values.

 Think of a time you felt connected to a colleague. How did you develop that connection?

You and parents

Teachers and parents are ultimately working towards the same purpose: to create the best learning experience for the child. You must consider that the students in your class come from differing family structures and backgrounds – this is why creating a sense of belonging that makes everyone feel connected is so important. Teachers and parents may have different ideas about what constitutes a 'good' education, about the 'right' way to teach and about the respective roles of teachers and parents. Find ways to acknowledge and talk through the differences. This will lay the foundations for ongoing conversations with parents which, in turn, helps students, who are caught between the worlds of home and school (Perkins, 2015).

Teacher–parent connection is critical to student success. Teachers need parents' support not only to share students' achievements, but to connect with what needs improvement. Student learning improves when teachers and parents connect.

Practical strategies to connect with parents include asking questions to get to know families and what their priorities are, establishing the best line of communication, and avoiding teacher jargon when communicating. Ensure your questions help broaden your understanding of the family's cultural background.

Be patient with yourself when it comes to managing parents and building these connections. To ensure mutual respect and understanding it is important to make parents feel welcome, listen to them and focus on their priorities, provide positive feedback rather than just reporting misbehaviour and keep them in the loop with timely personalised communication. This will lay the foundation for a collaborative approach to supporting their child's learning.

 Think of the people that you know. What do you do to connect with different people?

The connection to wellbeing

A healthy sense of belonging to your school and its community is underpinned by self-care. This is not selfish. Although self-care is about individual responsibility, it is not an entirely individual act (Ainsworth & Oldfield, 2019): it relies on relationships within all the ecosystems you will engage with during your early teaching career. This includes your family, school community, workplace, friends and culture. As an early career teacher, building connections to form relationships is everything. You will be exposed to all sorts of expectations from mentors, colleagues and parents, while concurrently managing all the other areas of your personal life: work, family, caring responsibilities, home duties, maintaining links with friends, travel and free time. This juggling act can help you to authentically develop as a professional, which is exciting, but this is also the time when your stress levels can considerably rise (Lemon & McDonough, 2020).

Let's take a look at some strategies for you to consider.

Actively reflect upon wellbeing

You probably feel like you're in a transition between feeling like a student but thinking like a teacher (Flores, 2020). You may think you do not have time to think about wellbeing, but you must make time. During your teaching career you will experience various critical moments that will require you to reflect upon your wellbeing routines. You will be navigating unknown and new relationships and finding your 'place'. If you don't pay attention to your wellbeing then increased stress levels, exhaustion, physical and mental stress may emerge. By developing and nurturing positive, honest and true-to-self connections within your school community, you start a journey of ongoing self-care to ensure your wellbeing is always catered for.

Know yourself

Enduring self-care relies on self-awareness. It is crucial to develop and nurture a safe space where you actively explore what wellbeing means to you and how to grow, maintain and protect it (Lemon, 2021). This is key to developing healthy relationships in the workplace and ultimately thriving as an early career teacher.

Self-care go-to box

A great way to manage your wellbeing in the diverse environments you work and live in is to develop a self-care go-to box. To begin with, think about self-care strategies that fit your style and personality, and record them – for example, by writing in a journal, mind mapping or recording your ideas on your phone. As you grow, you will add ideas and resources to your box. Over time it will be filled with diverse and personalised strategies that cover a variety of areas and activities that are critical to your wellbeing. Every person's go-to box will be different. For example, Celia uses mindfulness and meditation apps as well as relaxing music playlists, while Marghi uses walking in nature and calling her friends overseas. Throughout your career, as you journey through different school experiences, you may find that you need to evaluate your go-to box by adding, removing or rethinking strategies. Change ensures personal growth, which helps to sustain wellbeing.

Accept change and evolve

As you grow as a teacher, your sense of belonging to the profession will grow and naturally morph. Your teaching identity is fluid and multifaceted, and is shaped by negotiations, classroom practices and socio-cultural factors. Be compassionate and patient with yourself. Belonging, as a teacher, is an ongoing, ever-evolving process through which you need to be flexible and develop self-awareness to modify strategies as you go (Golzar, 2020). This will ensure your longevity in the profession. Giving yourself the opportunity to change may mean altering the environment you are in, not just you as a person. It may be that a school you have worked at no longer suits your teacher journey after a few years. It is okay to change and explore your options. Do not give up teaching just because you do not like the current teaching environment you are in. It's not that you don't like teaching anymore; you may just need a change of landscape.

Develop meaningful relationships

You need to give yourself time and opportunity to get to know the community, parents, students and staff at your school, and consider how you will manage the relationships between these various ecological environments while working in the school's ecosystem (Bronfenbrenner, 1979). This will support you both practically and emotionally to navigate possible challenges that impact how you feel about work. You can grow meaningful relationships through sharing who you are in your life, your interests and your dreams. Collaborative storytelling and discussion can empower early career teachers to preserve, share and achieve their ambitions (Lemon et al., 2022).

 **Let's reflect**

Reflecting upon yourself as a person

Belonging is a profound concept. It's strongly connected to wellbeing and contentment. It is impossible to separate a healthy sense of belonging as a person and as a professional, as the two are strongly interrelated. Therefore, it is critical that you reflect on your sense of belonging to be able to thrive holistically in all key levels of your life.

 What does belonging mean to you? How is belonging affected by different contexts? What do you do to show yourself compassion and to care for yourself?

Reflecting upon yourself as a professional

The AITSL Professional Standards, which guide our teaching practice and help us develop expertise, have a particular focus on belonging as a way of being and feeling valued in the community you work in. Let's focus on Standard 7, in the domain of Professional Engagement, which focuses on how we engage with colleagues, caregivers and members of the community.

 How does this relate to developing belonging to your profession in your school?

Reflect upon opportunities to engage in professional learning, with colleagues, parents and the community. Who in your school could you talk to about opportunities? What opportunities will you be more comfortable with? What are the areas of growth that will challenge you more?

Let's get practical

The best PD opportunity is literally down the hall: go and chat to an experienced teacher and ask for their advice, feedback and support.

Grab that cuppa and mingle in the staffroom – not just with your direct team, but also those who teach other subjects.

Begin to connect with other teachers who teach in areas that may not be your discipline or subject matter, but that you have a keen personal interest in, such as Languages or Sport – as well as those who teach in other year levels. This may improve your sense of belonging within the school community.

Do not think that you need to like everyone at school or that everyone will warm to you. It is natural to have affinities. Just seek the best in everyone and know that everyone will teach you something valuable.

Stay in touch with your university peers and the academics who helped you along the way. Sharing and caring is the best belonging of all, and networking in teaching is key.

Let's do something about it

If you had to provide a one to two-minute pitch describing who you are, your background, your experience, you vision and your teaching philosophy, what would you say? How would you introduce yourself?

Final words

As teachers in Australia, we are fortunate to live in a place rich in cultural wisdom. It is important that you embrace this to form deeper connections not only to where you live, but to culture as well. These connections will help you recognise and accept the ever-changing nature of your journey and develop a sense of belonging wherever you are. Education is a social process. Trust yourself, and use the time you have with others to develop attributes and qualities that will support you to continually grow into the teacher you want to be.

CHAPTER 2

I AM A SUCCESSFUL TEACHER

Learning is a process where knowledge is presented to us, then shaped through understanding, discussion and reflection.

– *Paulo Freire*

Celia's story

I spent my entre childhood playing 'schools' with my cousins and younger brother, mimicking my favourite teachers. School holidays were my favourite, as I got to act out a whole day. I even went as far as having my cousins and younger brother outside in the backyard for recess and lunch times, while I stayed in the kitchen pretending it was the staffroom. Being a teacher was part of who I was from as far back as I can remember.

Being accepted into my teaching degree was a great moment for me. I knew I was one step closer to achieving my dream. Being a successful teacher was always top of mind, but it was a learning curve to discover what that looked like, felt like and sounded like in the real world.

As I journeyed through my studies and, in particular, my teaching placements, I found myself continuously adjusting my ideas of what a successful teacher looked like based on the experiences I had, both negative and positive. I slowly started to build my own ideas of the teacher I wanted to be and what success looked like to me.

One of my mentor teachers on placement told me that successful teachers take the time to learn and use their students' names. This was one of the pieces of advice I popped into my successful teacher virtual toolbox. When I graduated and finally had my very own classroom, I walked into my first day with my toolbox and a plan. My plan was to learn and use my students' names. I could see immediately that my students felt a sense of comfort because of this.

Over the years I continued to build on my notion of what success as a teacher meant to me. While I continue to adjust this, I do have clarity around the question I pondered all those years ago: what does being a teacher look like, feel like and sound like in the real world? This is what I learnt: to me, a successful teacher looks to build connections with students and believes in their potential. A successful teacher feels empathy and listens with sensitivity to advise appropriately. A successful teacher sounds positive, prepared, patient and fair.

Writing your story

There are many ways to track your success as a teacher, yet most of them are immeasurable in their nature. There are so many factors that must be considered and combined to make a successful teacher. Think about the experiences you have had so far at university and in schools with mentors, teaching partners or colleagues.

- What is success to you? Think about two people who are not teachers and who you define as 'successful'. What makes them successful? How could you use some of their strengths in your teaching?
- Think about the best teacher you ever had. What did they do that you liked? What experiences would you add to your successful teacher virtual toolbox? How can you use your memories of this teacher to help you define what a 'successful' teacher means to you?

What experienced teachers say

Success as a teacher has many layers. Most often, teachers are judged by the results their students achieve. And although this is important and a key factor of your role, you can't achieve good results if you don't stop to think about how you are going to get them. Rote learning, drills and practice may keep parents happy, but for most students this has the opposite effect of what you're intending. Have a read of some of the strategies experienced teachers have used in their classrooms.

When I was a student myself, my mum asked me at the end of every school day, 'Did you listen to the teacher today?' It was just her way of checking in. As I grew older and she asked the same question, I remember thinking to myself, 'Yes, I listened, but did the teacher listen to me?' Of course, I kept this to myself; however it is something that had stuck with me. I wanted to ensure that if one of my students were ever asked whether their teacher listened to them, that they would respond with the feeling of being valued and appreciated. I took this experience from my own school days and used it to create a classroom where listening and mindfulness took priority. I would ensure that when I was listening to my students I would give them my full attention. I would ask open-ended questions and seek clarification. I would often paraphrase to ensure I understood what a student was asking me. – **Nicole**

Starting with the end in mind is a learning that has always been part of my practice. I walked into my first day of teaching with this as a goal. With each new lesson, I decided what I wanted my students to know or be able to do by the end. I would note this down in the form of a goal, where it was visible. I explained to my students what they would be learning and how they could show me what they learnt. I spent time practising with them and then gave them time to practise on their own or in groups. I gave them different options in the way they would practise, so that they could practise in a way that made sense to them. This helped me track each student's learning, and helped students track where they were with their learning. At the end of each lesson, I would give each student the opportunity to reflect on their success and use this to help them move forward with achieving the goal or setting a new one. – **Tanya**

> *As a graduate, I found that even the most motivated students could become demotivated and frustrated when they felt they weren't grasping a concept or even getting enough attention. I found that I spent most of my time dealing with the students who had more obvious challenges. I sought advice from colleagues and one of the strategies suggested to me was to provide opportunities for success by offering all students a chance to use their strengths and feel included. I realised at this point that I needed to get to know my students a little more before I could use this strategy. I did this through strength observation. I observed and noted who worked well in groups, what excited them, bored them, sustained their focus, what was challenging, what was easy. I even asked students to articulate their own strengths. – Kyle*

What is success?

Success as a teacher is what we'd refer to on social media as 'a complicated relationship'. Let's consider Bronfenbrenner (1979) and his theory of ecological systems again. As a teacher you will rely on all the elements of the ecosystem and the people in it to achieve success. Beneath the surface of success lie several foundational elements that underpin and contribute to achieving success. These underlying factors include:

- **competence** – beyond behaviour learnt during teacher training; includes critical thinking skills, reflective capabilities and a willingness to be on an ongoing, lifelong development journey
- **classroom practice** – connecting the Professional Standards to classroom work
- **connections** – with all stakeholders; working ethically, sensitively and collaboratively with students, parents, colleagues, external

professionals and community representatives to contribute to school life

- **professionalism** – maintaining the highest standards of professional conduct, aligning with the Professional Standards and maintaining your identity and integrity
- **commitment and self-efficacy** – belief in your skills and ability to lead to positive results and having the confidence and strength to keep learning from setbacks.

Passing your sense of success on

As a teacher you want nothing more than to support and motivate your students and colleagues to experience success in different aspects of their lives – from academic to social and emotional. Working on your own sense of success as a teacher and continuously building your competence, classroom practice, connections, professionalism and self-efficacy will be critical to pass your sense of success on.

You and your school

Successful teachers are invested in their school community both inside and outside the classroom. They get to know the community and environment around the school by being part of it. This can be as simple as supporting local businesses being represented in the school. Teachers are often seen as community leaders, so understanding the community in which you serve is crucial to your success. Conversely, the community can help you become a successful teacher. What you put into it, you get back. A range of studies that explored what makes successful teachers highlighted that the local setting of a school and its community may have a critical impact on teachers' classroom practices and, therefore, on student outcomes (Lee et al., 2012; Organisation for Economic Cooperation and Development, 2011). Local communities can inspire and contribute to effective and visionary instructional strategies, leadership, management and school governance, so get involved and you will reap the benefits.

 Think about a school community you have belonged to or currently belong to. What is your community's story?

You and your students

Your success begins with, and is forever connected to, the success of your students, and belief in your students is key to this. Believing in your students is one of the simplest but most powerful ways to have a positive impact on their learning. Your students are more likely to do better if they know you believe in them. To pass a sense of success on to your students it is important that you communicate expectations in a constructive way. The language you use to do this needs to motivate your students to believe they can participate in and contribute to their learning successfully, regardless of their ability level. Belief needs to be coupled with a supportive classroom environment where students feel valued and comfortable.

As your students are unique and diverse, try to use person-first language as most current inclusive education practices suggest. (For more guidance on person-first and inclusive language, refer to one of the many readily available language guides available from state and territory departments of education.) The way you talk to students can influence their success and, therefore, your own. It's important to speak to and about them positively.

Planning engaging and differentiated activities that reinforce and expand learning, without overloading or exhausting your students, is important to keep front of mind. Set goals with your students and work with them towards achieving those goals. Ultimately, the way you will do so will depend on the classrooms you have, so get to know your students and help them make their learning more 'visible'. As John Hattie (2011) says, rather than recommending a particular teaching method, teachers need to be evaluators of the effect of the methods that they choose.

 Think of a time someone believed in you. How did that support your success?

You and your colleagues

A successful teacher supports all colleagues, from front office staff to the people who clean your classrooms. Being a supportive colleague means that you are working collaboratively as part of a school community. You come to meetings prepared. You turn your attendance rolls and other requirements in on time. You are on time for yard duty. You leave your classroom tidy. If you take the time to support your colleagues you will earn their trust, and they'll know they can count on you. Being valued as a colleague is a sign of success.

There are many practical ways to make success visible with your colleagues. Perhaps create resource databases to share collective wisdom, lesson plans, rubrics and assessments. Observe your peers in action: sitting in their classroom as they interact with their students and providing them with instantaneous feedback is a sure-fire way to make success visible and create a culture of peer celebration and support.

 Think about a strength you have. How could you use this to support your teaching colleagues?

You and parents

As a teacher your ability to develop positive relationships with parents is an important aspect of your success. As a teacher you are accountable to parents as well as students. One of the ways you can develop great teacher–parent relationships is by communicating clearly and sensitively. Communication is a make-or-break skill as a teacher and it is crucial to success. Communication helps you to pass critical information and recommendations to parents that may be important to the student's success and wellbeing.

You will need to practise your listening skills to genuinely build an honest rapport: this is as simple as letting parents finish talking before interjecting, checking on their feelings first, using open-ended questions, and showing that you value their knowledge and understanding of their own children. With parents, as well as their children, use strength-based language and solutions: instead of focusing on what is not right or well done, focus on what is going well and how that could be used to better a challenging situation. A great way to connect with parents is to communicate promptly when their child achieves visible success with something at school, and avoid contacting them only when the child has a problem. A quick note to parents to let them know that their child had a win at school is a smart move.

 Think about your communication style in your personal and professional life. How can you differentiate your style to build professional relationships with your students' parents?

You and the profession

This aspect of sharing success is critical to cover in this chapter, as your success as a teacher is a success for the profession. You will evolve and grow as a teaching professional, and success will look different at each stage of your career. Yes, there will be assessment results and test scores, but it's also important to consider wellbeing at every level.

Success is a dynamic process, and its meaning will evolve and grow just like you will. If we as teachers think we have 'arrived' and there is nothing left to learn, this is when we may be left behind as our student cohorts will change over time, and so will their needs. It is key that you keep learning and evolving in all the areas that we have explored so far and that you engage in meaningful professional development.

From a Professional Standards viewpoint, success will occur when you progressively move from graduate level to proficient, highly accomplished up to lead.

 What are some examples of professional development you would like to explore in this early stage of your career?

The connection to wellbeing

Wellbeing is about much more than having coping mechanisms to employ in negative situations. It encompasses ideas about what it means to live a happy and content life. Wellbeing leads to success. Wellbeing is multidimensional, comprising physical, mental, emotional and spiritual aspects. It is about feeling content and functioning well in both your professional and personal life. Being able to make your own connections between your success and wellbeing is important as a teacher. Here are some tips to help you along the way.

Reconnect to your purpose and focus on your goals

Try to do one thing each week that reminds you why you became a teacher in the first place. Use a teaching strategy that you and your students all enjoy, which will remind you of the difference you're making in their lives. Setting goals is a great way to give you direction, focus and motivation. Try to ensure that all your goals are achievable, measurable and have an end point. It can be helpful to break a larger goal into more manageable bite-sized goals. Think of something that, if you do it today, will make you feel satisfied and accomplished.

Adopt a growth mindset in your teaching

There's great value in trying new things and accepting mistakes as opportunities to learn. We could all do with a reminder of the power of 'yet' – that is, 'I haven't quite mastered this skill *yet*'. It can be helpful to see yourself as a learner (just like your students) and to spend time reflecting on new ideas, considering what you have learnt and acknowledging areas that you find challenging. Ensuring you have healthy coping skills can help in times of stress. We'll talk more about adopting a growth mindset in Chapter 6.

Focus on kindness and gratitude

An act of appreciation or kindness supports positive emotions, stronger social connections and improved wellbeing. Consider simple ways you can build gratitude and kindness into your day. And the best thing? Kindness and gratitude are contagious, so imagine the benefit to your classroom.

Create clear boundaries between home and school

Set a reasonable time for leaving school each day (and stick to it). Find ways to turn off your teacher mindset so that you can relax when you get home. Try to balance your teacher identity with your out-of-school identity. Can you make time once a week for a hobby or sport that you value? How can you put boundaries around the time you spend working in the evenings and on weekends?

Set up effective debriefing and mentoring structures

Teaching can be an emotionally taxing job that throws up many different challenges. Set up structures that help you to focus on solutions rather than problems. While a venting session may make you feel better in the short term, it doesn't solve the problem and may keep you feeling stuck. Consider using a debriefing structure to help manage your thinking about challenging situations – for example, team up with a supportive colleague and set up a formal mentor relationship structure.

Build up emotional resilience and reward yourself

Think of proactive ways to manage the stress in your life. Meet regularly with friends and family, spend time on hobbies you enjoy, read, or watch things that make you laugh. Build proven stress-busting activities into your daily routine – consider yoga, meditation or exercises that involve deep breathing. Perhaps join a team sport or start a walking practice. Consider teaming up with another teacher to become 'wellbeing buddies', and discuss how you can support each other – for example, having regular check-ins or going for a short walk together at lunchtime. The improved physical and psychological health that comes from prioritising your wellbeing is a reward, but there's also value in using tangible rewards when you meet goals. Consider simple and practical ways to reward yourself whenever you reach a goal. For example, plan a mini getaway, enjoy a good book or movie, have a social gathering or buy yourself a gift.

 **Let's reflect**

Reflecting upon yourself as a person

Success can be a visible, celebratory event, moment or result, as well as a feeling. The way we 'feel' success is different for everyone, based on our personality and history, as well as our needs and expectations. This is when you need to reflect upon any biases you hold about yourself, and any sense of imposter syndrome that may affect your ability to see and celebrate success when it happens.

 What does success mean to you? What are your success habits?

Reflecting upon yourself as a professional

When we talk about being successful as a teacher and compliance to the Professional Standards, we cannot really pinpoint a specific standard to focus on more than another. Success encompasses all the Professional Standards. The AITSL standards are indeed like building blocks that enable teachers to develop knowledge and skills across various domains. Your success will stem from the holistic interactions of these standards once enabled in your professional practice. Therefore, let's refer to the three domains underpinning all the Professional Standards: Professional Knowledge, Professional Practice and Professional Engagement.

 What might success look like for you in each of these domains at the end of your first teaching year?

Which one is your strength and which one do you feel you need to work on further?

 ## Let's get practical

As Hattie's visible learning theory says, you need to use evidence-based approaches to keep evaluating your work (Hattie, 2011). Match your weekly teaching to the AITSL Professional Standards in your planning documents. Practise using the standards' focus areas to map your work. This will help make your own learning visible and change your direction if you do not see specific focus areas used as much as others. It would be very useful to do this with the help of a senior peer, your teaching partner or mentor, who can coach and guide you.

 ## Let's do something about it

Try to regularly write down three good things that have happened while at school. They can be small or big things. It may be a smile or thank you from a challenging student or witnessing an 'aha' moment when a student has grasped a concept. At the end of the week, review your list and congratulate yourself on a job well done. This will help you get into the habit of seeing the positive rather than being preoccupied with the negative.

Final words

Success is a dynamic and multifaceted process of growth. Your teaching journey will comprise of celebrations, reflections, lightbulb moments and multiple setbacks. Your choices create your path and shape your experiences. There are no set routes – you ultimately create your own map as you navigate your way through. Your success will be as unique and special as you are. Ambiguity and uncertainty will be your friends; so will self-awareness. Embracing these can lead to positive outcomes or insights. There will be achievements along the way but there must be an element of being wrong or not succeeding. This is how you grow. If you are always right and surrounded by people who do not challenge you, then you are in the wrong place. As a teacher, you must always be learning.

CHAPTER 3

I CAN REALLY BE MYSELF AT THIS SCHOOL

The self is not something ready-made, but something in continuous formation through choice of action.

– John Dewey

Luc's story

From the start of my teaching career, I decided that it was key for me to share with students the importance of being yourself and finding your identity. Nevertheless, this was also very challenging for me as I had spent years of my teaching career unable to disclose a part of my own identity. From my LGTBQI+ perspective, my identity isn't always easy to discuss in a profession often challenged by conservative bureaucracy.

Separating our personal and professional lives is crucial in developing appropriate teacher–student relationships, and I always was guided by this. But as a secondary teacher, I felt responsible to be honest and open about my identity with my students. While students don't need every detail about your life, your identity is something that can help you develop bonds with your students. This is especially true in the secondary school years. Your students themselves are at the point of working out what their own identities are and how they fit in.

When the same-sex marriage plebiscite happened in Australia, I felt that this was the time for me to start discussions with my colleagues and principals and to use this real-world example to discuss legislation with my senior students. At first this did cause some debate with parents; however, my colleagues and school leadership supported me in figuring out what to discuss and what not to discuss within my classroom. By now, word had gotten out that I may belong to the LGTBQI+ community, but I had not confirmed or denied this. It was during this time that I was approached by two of my students. They were at first unsure if they should let me know what they had been hearing in the schoolyard, but with a big gasp of a breath they let it out. They told me that they had heard whispers that I was gay.

The moment I was terrified of was staring me in the face. I was flooded with thoughts of being fired, students losing respect for me and parents taking their children out of my classes because of my identity. I quickly gathered my thoughts and responded the best way I could, guided by my belief in being open and honest. I asked, 'Do you know what gay means?' They both nodded. 'Well then, I am gay,' I replied. And that's where my story began. The students smiled and told me that another one of their favourite teachers was also gay. Instead of equating the word 'gay' with 'weird' or a joke between friends, they now equated it with someone they knew as their teacher. Someone who owned their identity, and someone who could help other LGTBQI+ students feel supported, safe and encouraged to learn.

Writing your story

Authenticity emerges from understanding what's important to you and remaining true to your values and beliefs in the face of any external pressure. When you come from a place that is authentic, you are less likely to allow these external pressures to change who you truly are. In saying this, schools are communities where everyone has rights and duties. There will be times when you need to negotiate and balance your needs with those of the colleagues, parents and students around you.

Choosing the right school setting is important to helping you be your authentic self; it is key to helping build your competence, classroom practice, connections, professionalism and self-efficacy, as discussed in Chapter 2. Being authentic is what makes you a great teacher and will help with continuous development.

Think back to Chapter 1, and about the image you hold of yourself in relation to entering a school setting for the first time. Now, let's extend this further and reflect on your authentic self.

What do you value most in your life? What beliefs of yours, if any, are set in stone?

What would those who know you best say about you and who you are?

How comfortable would you feel in sharing your thoughts about unpopular or controversial topics?

What experienced teachers say

It is important to remember that being your authentic self as a teacher is something that evolves with practise, over time. It extends further than demonstrating your teacher knowledge; it also involves creating strong relationships with students through genuine interactions. Have a read of what experienced teachers say about authenticity.

> *Being approachable is something that is important in developing relationships with your students, and this is something that is core to my identity as a person and teacher. Simple things such as learning students' names, asking them what they like to be called, setting expectations and giving students the opportunity to be involved in this can develop an environment of trust.*
> *– Joshua*

> *Being a storyteller and using real-world narratives, whether they belong to you or are general, can support students to connect with you, their peers, and their everyday lives. Of course, we need to always ensure we are balancing the personal information we share, but by sharing both positive experiences and, at times, our struggles we can improve a student's emotional connection to us. – Eva*

> *When students can see that you have a genuine love and care for teaching and learning this can be inspiring to them. One way of achieving this is to focus on a student's learning and not just the content you need to cover. Explain concepts over and over. This will show students you care about them learning and not just getting through content. – **Lamia***

What is authenticity?

Authenticity is often described as being and acting 'real' and 'genuine'. When we reflect upon authenticity as teachers, we are often advised to 'just do what comes naturally'. But it's not that simple. Much deeper complexities frequently hide popular definitions and superficial advice, and that is the case with authenticity.

Researchers from the University of Edinburgh wrote a literature review about authenticity in the teaching profession (Kreber, 2010). They noted that there is a problem with the advice to 'be real' and 'do what comes naturally': this assumes that you, as a teacher, know your real self and how to act in ways that are consistent with that self. In reality, knowledge of self does not come easily. It must be discovered, learned and developed over time. For many teachers, this takes effort – it did for us, and still is an ongoing journey. Nevertheless, the effort to achieve authenticity in teaching is worth pursuing. Teachers who share what is genuine and real about themselves challenge students to also explore their own authenticity. This is teaching that goes beyond changing what students know: it can change who they are.

Authenticity is underpinned by feeling comfortable with who you are, being accepted into a particular group that resonates with you and staying true to your values and beliefs. It is a type of confidence that doesn't come from obtaining something *outside* of yourself; rather, it emerges from deeply knowing that you are 'enough'. Whatever your feelings, needs or skills and whatever you do, you are enough, and you can make a difference. You can stay true to your own personality, essence and character despite many pressures, which, let's be honest, will always be there.

Authenticity is one of the most important ingredients in creating healthy and sustainable professional relationships. Yet it can also be one of the most challenging to practise on a day-to-day basis, and may also impact heavily on the decisions you make regarding which school contexts you want to work in. Authenticity in teaching is complex and multidimensional. It involves being real, honest and self-aware, and being defined by your own expectations rather than others'. It also requires you to bring parts of yourself into your interactions with the school community. Authenticity hinges on your ability to critically reflect on yourself, others, your relationships, and the context in which you work and live. Authenticity is 'not just something that exclusively rests within [yourself] ... for authenticity to be meaningful it needs to be sought in relation to issues that matter crucially' (Kreber et al. 2007, p. 41).

Passing your sense of self on

Authenticity is a process that supports genuine professional connections and allows for meaningful relationships to be built between yourself and everyone who operates in the school ecosystem. It is important to remember that while some of your values and beliefs will be flexible and adaptable, and may change over time, others are essential to who you are and are very difficult to shift – and neither should they. You may have core values and beliefs related to religion, politics and social or economic status. You may also have key values regarding family, culture and even your physical appearance. These are major principles that, if compromised, will impact your authentic self.

You and your school

As we've discussed, a school is an ecosystem: 'a biological community of interacting organisms and their physical environment' according to the *Oxford English Dictionary*. In the ecosystem you will encounter various people with their own values and beliefs. Some will be embedded deeply and strongly influence the school community. If your values differ, this may scare you; you may feel vulnerable. Especially when you are new to a school, you may be afraid that if you share specific thoughts or experiences you will create conflict, distance and misunderstandings. You may feel the urge to totally conform to the strongest group or speak up all the time to reaffirm yourself.

It is important to realise that authenticity is a personal journey that requires compassion and tolerance. How you choose to be authentic will be quite different from how your colleague, your principal, your students and their parents choose to be so. You may believe that your clothing and hairstyle are critical to reflecting your authenticity; while someone else may focus on family life, for example, and may find it important to bring children or pets into their workplace at times. Others may choose to honour their cultural heritage with artifacts such as arts or foreign language posters and cards set on display in their office space.

These days, the challenge in schools, like other workplaces, is how to foster a context that encourages authenticity. What can a principal do to capitalise from existing diverse perspectives? In your career, it is critical that you find a school community that resonates with you; a context that manages diverse perspectives in a way that allows the school community to be efficient and thrive, despite the differences. In our 21st-century society, more than ever, this is going to require courage and collaboration.

The most authentic schools are those where all stakeholders are unafraid to engage with conversations that can be difficult and uncomfortable and that are open to negotiation, and where they are willing to do the work to address perspectives that do not always suit the community or uphold the status quo. These schools encourage innovative conversations and whole-system changes, with the result that teachers are more confident and engaged because they feel they can bring their true selves into their workplace.

Taking on this challenge will help you develop intercultural under-standing and socio-emotional learning, and will also allow you to model this to students. Remember, authenticity is a journey, and no one can tell you where it should lead you. Being authentic, with others and to yourself, might be the bravest thing you have ever done.

 What small step could you take today to make you feel more authentic in the classroom? What would make your work context more engaging? What would make you feel more authentic?

You and your students

Teachers who have an authentic teaching style are more positively received by their students. To achieve a more authentic style, take time to talk with students and their families, seeking opportunities to share experiences. This means viewing teaching as an opportunity for an ongoing dialogue between you as the teacher and the wider school community. Authentic teachers demonstrate a willingness to share something about their life when appropriate and share elements of their humanity by telling personal stories and jokes and, at times, by admitting mistakes. Authentic teachers demonstrate care and compassion towards students by recognising them as individuals and attending to their needs both academically and personally (Johnson and LaBelle, 2017).

As a teacher, you need to establish boundaries between your personal life and work. Being authentic at school does not mean you have to share every single detail of your personal life. Occasionally, as teachers, you may share stories about your family or pets, for example, but always be careful to not overshare information and ensure that you are not making others feel uncomfortable.

An interpersonal and genuine approach to teaching sees the learning experience holistically. As a teacher, it is critical to approach your teaching from a reflective standpoint, periodically checking in on how *you* would like to be taught and how this might differ from your colleagues, your students, their parents and the whole school community. It is important you trace back to what teaching and learning means to you.

 What might be some authentic, appropriate personal stories that you could share with your students to display who you are? What could guide your decision-making in relation to when or what to share? For example, when you're teaching about different cultures, could you share something about your own heritage?

You and your colleagues

Building authentic professional teacher relationships with your colleagues is important for longevity and professional development. Sharing your passions, stories, good practices and learnings with your colleagues and those in your wider network will support you in developing genuine relationships. Through this process you will learn that you will have many similarities with your colleagues, the most prominent being that teachers are self- aware professionals who have made a commitment to teaching and continually reflect on the purpose of education. Many of your colleagues will share your same discipline or specialisation areas. Try to involve your colleagues in something you are passionate about, and that may extend your discipline knowledge base. If you are working on a project yourself, be that for university or for your classroom, show colleagues your own work in progress and ask for their input. Authenticity finds expression in consistency between values and actions. This should empower your relationships with your colleagues, even when there are conflicts: at a values level, you come from the same place.

 Think of a time your felt connected to a colleague. How did you develop that connection? What's one thing you could share about yourself with a colleague that might spark a more meaningful connection with them?

You and parents

A good place to start thinking about authentic teaching is to consider your own teaching philosophy and speak explicitly about it with your students' parents. Being transparent about what motivates you in your teaching demonstrates self-awareness, which is fundamental to both teaching and learning. This helps you create trust and respect.

One way you could share your teaching philosophy is to find opportunities to relate stories, anecdotes and even projects you and your colleagues may be working on. You may ask your colleagues if they are interested in holding an information evening where you share this. These sessions can help parents ask clarifying questions about how your teaching supports their child's learning, and can help you build authentic relationships with parents that allow you to co-construct the learning environment. Remember, each parent's way of being authentic may be informed by different values, experiences and expectations to your own.

 Think of the people you know in your personal life. What do you do to connect with different types of people?

The connection to wellbeing

The first important thing to reflect upon is your 'threshold of authenticity', which is the level of genuine engagement that has the most impact on your wellbeing and represents the satisfaction of feeling true to yourself. Think about a time when you felt fully engaged; when you thought: 'This is my moment. I feel real, I feel myself.' How can you ensure you have more of those moments? Authenticity is not about uncovering your soul and every single private detail of your life. It is about identifying what's important to you and how you can integrate that into your professional life so that you can experience satisfaction, feel engaged, and make a positive contribution to work and society.

Authenticity is interpersonal and relies on emotional intelligence, respect, listening and a lot of compassion and understanding. Authenticity is both a personal journey and a relational process. It involves ongoing critical reflection and adaptation. In the context of wellbeing, authenticity means alignment, which means that you align your thoughts, emotions, and actions with who you truly are, the core of your identity. This allows you to be filled with enthusiasm, have a sense of purpose and find meaning in all you do. When your genuine self comes through in all you do in your personal and professional life, that is authentic empowerment (Zukav, 1999). Here are some strategies to enhance your authentic self in your school community.

Share about yourself, but be clear on boundaries

If you have an interest, hobby, aptitude, family members or pets that you really love, build the trust and share accordingly. As a teacher, however, there are boundaries related to compliance. Always ensure no students or colleagues can see your social media accounts and be extremely responsible of what you post publicly. Being a teacher demands high responsibility in digital communication.

Find your tribe

Your interests are also someone else's interests – be that reading, theatre, charitable community work, marathons or movies, just to name a few. Finding your tribe is important. It can start in the staffroom by sitting down with various people over a chat. Finding connections with colleagues will support you in relating to others' perspectives and ideas, and in developing healthy work relationships.

Be inspired, not a duplication

As a graduate teacher, it is tempting to duplicate the lessons the teacher in the next room developed and believe that this will make you as successful as them. However, this can have the opposite effect – it can block you from bringing your authentic personal self to your teaching. It's tempting to emulate amazing teachers, but to become that distinctive teacher you are meant to be, and to share your unique experience and passion with the school community, you must experiment with those great ideas you may have percolating in your mind; only this way you will experience 'magic' happening in your classroom (Dabbs & Howard, 2015).

Share your emotions

You might have heard the saying, 'Don't smile until Easter,' meaning stay composed with your students to show your authority. Well, we encourage you to do the opposite! Smile, laugh, frown and maybe even cry well before Easter. Teachers are humans and humans have emotions. By expressing your emotions in a healthy way, you model to your students how to convey and regulate human emotions. It's perfectly fine for your students to see you frown when you're frustrated or light up when they walk in the room.

Verbally labelling your feelings for your students is great learning moment. 'I'm frustrated that you all left the class an absolute mess yesterday after assembly!' or 'I'm really worried today because my dog isn't well.' When you make a mistake, admit it and laugh about it, demonstrate how you're correcting it and, if needed, apologise. This will also model metacognitive skills – that is, how you go about learning yourself, while also naming and recognising emotions as they arise.

Another option for bringing authenticity to the classroom is via humour. Explore ways that resonate with you personally that may bring some lightheartedness into the classroom. There are many ways to be fun and light. Obviously, you should also be aware of cultural differences among your students when it comes to what is considered 'funny' or not so much.

 ## Let's reflect

Reflecting upon yourself as a person

To be authentic while also maintaining your professional self, always take some time to reflect on how these suggestions might help you bring your true self to school while also keeping comfortable boundaries. Simple changes in how you present yourself, how you speak and how you open up in diverse ways will help your students get to know you as a real person.

 What are your non-negotiable values and beliefs?

How do you balance your values and beliefs with those of others?

In what situations do you find it difficult to be authentic? Why is that? What would happen if you tried to show a bit more of how you really feel in those situations?

Reflecting upon yourself as a professional

If you visit the AITSL Professional Standards website, you can do a quick search using the key terms 'authentic' and 'authenticity'. You will see they are associated with the importance of collecting evidence of your practice and the importance of selecting and using valid technology in your classroom work. Reflect on the potential and impact on your classroom practice as an early career educator. In particular, think about the relevance of Standards 1 and 2, in the domain of Professional Knowledge, which relate to knowing how students learn and how to teach your content.

 How does knowing your students and the way they learn encourage authentic learning experiences?

How can you provide authentic learning contexts within your discipline/s? This will extend not just to the lesson you build and design, but also the data that you collect as evidence of your practice.

Let's get practical

Think about how you can create a welcoming space in your classroom that considers the diverse cultural needs of learners. Your classroom needs to be appropriately humanised as much as possible. All students need to feel welcomed and that the environment they are in is conducive to their learning needs. One way of doing this is to ensure you get to know each student's strengths and background and show them they are valued.

As much as you can, plan learning that involves real-world problems or situations in your school's community. You can do this with your colleagues to support building ideas, and with your students to support them in being motivated to produce work that has an authentic audience. For example, start a newspaper or email newsletter for school families to communicate school and local news and events.

Where appropriate, think about giving students in your classroom the opportunity to make choices on how they would like to learn something and how they would like to demonstrate their learning. You can offer options and support their choices.

 ## Let's do something about it

Take the time to think about how you can build school community partnerships and connect this to your teaching. Taking a community walk could be a good start. It could help you survey your community's resources and identify possible partner opportunities. By deepening your understanding of the community your school exists within, you will begin to build a true understanding of the cultural and socio-economic needs of the families in your school and can use this to support you in finding your authentic professional self.

Final words

If you ever, in your profession, find yourself feeling disempowered, or if you're lacking enthusiasm, purpose or meaning, is it possible that you're living out of alignment with your true self? At times it may be challenging to hold onto your dreams and ideals, or you may find that they are changing – and that is fine. It may be confusing, but through self-reflection, you can embrace who you are and evolve in your professional and personal journey. Always remember you are capable of change, and at times you will need to action those changes to continue your journey authentically.

CHAPTER 4

I AM GOOD AT HELPING STUDENTS LEARN NEW THINGS

The teacher's role is not to teach but to help the child learn.

– *Maria Montessori*

Ebony's story

I began my first year feeling quite confident about being able to help students achieve their learning goals. However, as a 23-year-old, in my first year out I was given a Year 11 General Mathematics class with 26 students, 25 of whom were energetic boys. I was teaching in a low socio-economic school with most students in my class being EAL/D students. As you can imagine, engaging this many students with diverse needs in a typical classroom, while covering quite difficult mathematical concepts, was not easy. I needed to reassess my classroom strategies very quickly to ensure every student in my class was supported – all 26 of them!

The first thing I did was think about the learning climate. We were within four walls, with very little natural light, and usually the class was in the middle of the day when students were bursting with energy. The second thing I did was think about how I was engaging with these students. I was frustrated they were not listening, or understanding the concepts I was teaching them. Our next unit was trigonometry, and the first topic was Pythagoras's theorem – I was dreading chalk and talk, and knew this was the time to change things up. My approach up to this point had not been effective, and my students were disengaged.

So, I did something quite bold for a VCE Mathematics class (at the time, at least – some 20 years ago) and took the students outside. Instead of telling them about the concepts, we explored them. I was so worried about the students making noise, or it is looking like my class was disruptive and that I was not in control. As a first-year teacher, this is one of the scariest situations to be in. However, I found that by making concepts real, taking them off a whiteboard and showing them in real contexts, my students could visualise and make sense of the theories behind what we were doing – they were engaged! We used our bodies to create triangles, and used long wooden rulers to measure our lengths, to prove the theorem $c^2 = a^2 + b^2$. The fresh air, light and fun we had all added to the experience. I found that not only were the students able to understand the concepts better, but we also built positive relationships at the same time. Feedback from the students was so positive, and they all excelled in their assignment, being able to correctly apply the theorem in all situations.

I knew from this point on in my teaching career that there was more I needed to consider to make my teaching effective. I needed to create a positive learning environment. This doesn't always need to be outside; it just needs to be suitable and relevant for the learning goals, and for your students. Always consider practical applications. It is important to connect with your students, and get to know them and how they learn best – every student is different. You need to have reasonable expectations of your students, their behaviour and abilities and most important you need to have a sense of humour and show this to your students. And don't ever be afraid to try something different if what you are trying is not working. Showing students you are willing to explore and learn new things is great role modelling.

Writing your story

Think back to when you were at school and of a teacher who had the most impact on you when you were learning something new. Reflect on the models or strategies that they used that were effective at helping you learn new things.

 Of what you remember, what were the most important things they did?

How did their strategies motivate and support your learning of new concepts?

What experienced teachers say

Helping students learn new things should be a teacher's priority. Understanding that this looks different for each student is at the core of effectively being able to do this. For some of your students, success at learning something new might look like getting good grades. For others, it might be about how involved they are in a classroom activity. As teachers it is important to know your students and use that knowledge to create learning experiences that help them learn new things. Following are a few examples from experienced teachers.

> It has taken me time to apply this consistently, but this is my go-to strategy to teach new things: the 'I Do, We Do, You Do' model. I am sure you have seen this strategy used in classrooms during your professional experiences. I start with demonstrating (I Do) – for example, how to use full stops to write a sentence – then I invite the students to write a sentence with me (We Do). Finally, I ask students to have a go writing a sentence on their own (I Do). Students who are still at the We Do stage can be invited to work with me as part of a small group. This is such a simple strategy that can be flexibly adapted to any school level, from early childhood up to Year 12.
> – *Pauline*

> Varying ways of teaching the same concept is part of my thinking when planning to teach something new and potentially challenging. Ensuring that I give students different options in the way they learn allows for greater opportunity for learning to happen. At times I tend to overcomplicate things, so having someone to check in with (like a colleague) helps. Don't think you can be a master of diversification from the get-go – it takes time, and you need to find what suits you and your students best.

To apply diversification, you must understand your students' different learning needs, likes and dislikes. It is from this I have been able to plan activities around different preferences and strengths. For example, instead of standing at the front of the classroom talking to the students for half the lesson, I would have stations set up around the classroom that incorporate learning new things, visually, by listening, through reading and writing and physically. Experimenting with new ways and seeing what works and what doesn't makes our teaching a bit more exciting as well. – Kelly

Consistently establishing goals and monitoring them for your students can be one of the most challenging and time-consuming tasks among the varying other duties a teacher has, but it does make a huge difference when it comes to teaching new things and reporting on them. I have had to work hard throughout my career to develop goal- setting strategies, and I have often had to remind myself I need to be flexible, as goal-setting may need to change depending on the students we have, the school we are in, the class level, curriculum and so forth. However, from my experience, having a consistent and manageable approach to goal-setting really helped me support my students to learn new things. Setting goals (especially starting with manageable chunks and then elevated big goals) always allows me to build a student's knowledge from the stage of understanding a new concept they are at. I often involve students in setting the goals and give them steps they can follow to work towards the goal. This may help them be involved in the progress they make with learning something new, and can start from as early as kindergarten and preschool. – Jamie

What does it mean to help students learn new things?

Being able to teach new things successfully relates to what we would define as 'effective teaching'. Being an 'effective' teacher is what all educators aim for – it is at the core of what we do. You may think teaching is solely about knowing your subject matter or content and how to teach it. However, this is only part of it. We discussed in earlier chapters that school communities are diverse and that learning needs vary greatly. AITSL Standard 1, knowing your content and how to teach it, is dependent on the teacher understanding the diverse needs within their classroom so they can help students learn new things. Effective teaching is an ongoing journey of developing knowledge and skills, applying them, delivering them, adapting them to diverse audiences, and then developing them again at various levels in a continuous cycle of improvement.

Self-efficacy is another concept we explored earlier, and this plays an important part in effectively teaching your students new things. Recent research says that that those teachers who have high levels of self-efficacy – that is, those who believe in their own abilities – have the biggest impact on student learning (Thornton et al., 2020). Bandura's theory of self-efficacy posits that our sense of self-efficacy and belief in our ability to control our practice provides the foundation for motivation, wellbeing and personal success (1997). Self-efficacy makes us more resilient to stress and challenges and it is the basis for motivation, which encourages us to apply and further our learning and pass this on to our learners. Although you cannot always influence the contexts in which you teach, you can have an influence on teaching effectiveness by believing in your abilities and allowing this to guide you to be best version of your teacher self.

Passing self-efficacy on

One thing to remember is that self-efficacy is not about having the skills to complete a particular task – it is about *believing* you can. Your belief in your ability to achieve an outcome or accomplish a goal will directly impact how you manage it. With this in mind, let's take a look at how modelling self-efficacy benefits the entire school ecosystem.

You and your school

Personal teacher attributes and a sense of self-efficacy can increase not only your ability to help students learn new things, but can also deeply impact your wellbeing – especially when it comes to how you feel perceived as a teacher in a school community. Working on developing your self-efficacy and using it in your practice can support you in having a positive presence in the school community. We explored Bronfenbrenner's ecological systems theory in Chapter 1, in relation to belonging. We can apply this again to self-efficacy. The sense the school community has about you is directly related to the image of yourself you project to the world. Passing on your sense of self-efficacy will satisfy your fundamental need as a teacher to demonstrate that you are good at teaching your students new things.

A positive educational culture that encourages and supports you is key to your ongoing growth, and that of your learners. Don't think you need to do this all on your own. You can contribute to such a culture, but you must be supported in this process. As AITSL says:

> Performance and development is about creating a culture of teacher quality, feedback and growth ... The quality of teaching is the most significant in-school factor affecting student outcomes, and there is strong evidence that better appraisal and feedback leading to targeted development can improve teacher performance. Professional growth is supported through a strong professional learning culture.' (AITSL, n.d. b).

Always reflect upon your own skills and knowledge and how you can contribute to your school's efficacy, but also seek support when you need to.

 Think about a school where you taught or currently teach. Consider how your self-efficacy played a role in how you were perceived as a teacher in that school community.

You and your students

To be able to teach students to learn new things, they must feel, deep inside, that you believe they can. This is also true for teachers. Students must believe their teacher can teach them new things. It's through communicating your self-efficacy that your students will have confidence in you.

Building self-efficacy in your students is crucial to them becoming competent learners. Modelling, and leading by example through your delivery, is key. Encouraging students to succeed in a task is perhaps one of the most important things you can do. This does not mean giving students easy tasks that don't challenge them. Tasks need to be challenging but supported by scaffolding, time allowance and even breaking tasks down into smaller, more manageable steps. Once a student is confident with the content you've just introduced, their self-efficacy will be enhanced and their motivation to keep learning increases. Therefore, ensuring that you set achievable tasks for students needs to be part of your thinking when planning activities.

Clarity of goals is also key to building a student's self-efficacy. To ensure students make the most of your teaching, you need to align your teaching to clear learning goals (Barbeau & Cornejo Happel, 2023). This will help you dispel any anxiety, reach measurable outcomes, create solid assessment tasks and give meaningful feedback. Be as clear as you can about your lesson goals – always try to define and communicate desired outcomes for your students. Repeat them from one lesson to the next, and even display them. Research says that students appreciate clear instructions and effective planning, but how this looks depends on the students you are teaching. A primary classroom may be quite different to a secondary or early childhood setting. Your students are the deciding factor, and are never too young to start being agents of their own learning. The ground rule for early career teachers is: keep it simple. If you try to cover too many 'things' you will get lost and so will your learners. Remember to be approachable when it comes to being asked questions and providing instructional and emotional support (Graham et al., 2022): if students feel safe asking questions, then learning new things will become a less daunting and more enjoyable process.

 Think of the last time you planned and taught a lesson. What did you do throughout to keep the students motivated to persist with learning the new content?

You and your colleagues

Strong and healthy relationships among teachers is seen as an essential aspect of school effectiveness as well as career enhancement (AITSL, 2022). Teacher collegiality can impact your professional growth and job satisfaction, especially in the early stages of your career. It can also impact your professional commitment, which in turn affects student performance and outcomes.

It is important that you seek occasions to be collegiate with your colleagues. When we speak of collegiality here we don't just mean collaboration or going out socially. We encourage you to engage with your teaching peers on many levels: talk about classroom practice, engage in frequent conversations about how they teach, plan and assess new content. Find occasions to observe other teachers in class and ask clarifying questions, especially when they are teaching new content. When it comes to the curriculum, find ways to plan, design, research and evaluate together. If you have someone you look up to, ask them to share what they know about teaching, learning and leading. Listening to their story about their craft is important and can support you in building and sharing your self-efficacy.

 Think of a time you engaged with your peers at university or colleagues in your workplace to learn something new. How did that support you in building and sharing your self-efficacy?

You and parents

Like with your students, being positive, clear, organised and the best teacher version of yourself also applies to your interactions with parents. Demonstrating that you care for their children's learning and that you believe their children are capable of persisting when new content is introduced is key to build a trusting relationship with parents and passing your sense of self-efficacy on. Positive teacher–parent communication benefits everyone: you, parents, students and the whole school community. Clear communication on your goals regarding new content and involving parents on how they can practically help will support you in building your self-efficacy. Think about how you can incorporate good two-way communication channels beyond parent-teacher interviews. Think about how student portfolios, emails or even once-a-term open classroom afternoons can support this. These types of positive interactions with parents can demonstrate how the class is progressing through learning and engaging in the lessons. Be creative but remember to always align with the school ethos and practices.

When communicating with parents about their child's learning, keep it simple and focus on classroom activities and goals, the child's accomplishments and challenges, and how parents can help. Parents need to feel represented and valued and want to know that their child's teacher understands how to best teach them new things.

Think of some parents you have crossed paths with at school. How did you interact with them to demonstrate your sense of self-efficacy in relation to teaching their child?

The connection with wellbeing

As you move through your early years as a teacher and effectively teach new things to your students, your self-efficacy will increase. Research indicates that self-efficacy is a significant factor for your wellbeing, because you feel prepared and capable, and can cope in various situations. Teacher self-efficacy is positively related to academic outcomes and teachers' wellbeing, satisfaction, commitment and accomplishment (Xiyun et al., 2022). On the other hand, lack of self-efficacy has detrimental effects on student outcomes and on your mental health. The higher your self-efficacy, the more improvement you will see in your life satisfaction, resilience when there are issues at school, and social inclusion. Along the way you will go through trials and make mistakes. Be patient with yourself. You need self-efficacy to teach effectively in a sustained manner, and it will grow with practice and genuine self-reflection.

It is critical to realise that self-efficacy is different but related to self-esteem. Self-esteem is a realistic respect in your ability to thrive in life, while self-efficacy is your belief in what you can accomplish. You may have a healthy self-esteem but a lower self-efficacy, or vice versa. If you work on both, you will achieve great balance at work and at home. Experts say that by increasing your self-efficacy, you may also increase your self-esteem as you allow yourself to succeed in life through motivation, commitment and optimism, without prematurely giving up on your goals.

Let's look at some ways to build your self-efficacy as an early career teacher.

Set flexible goals

Set yourself reasonable goals that are achievable and measurable. When teaching new content to students, be as clear to them as you are with yourself on the outcomes you want to achieve. Be realistic and readjust your desired outcomes as you go along. This way you will be using your self-efficacy to enhance your self-confidence about your ability to follow through.

Check your emotions

Observe your emotions, thoughts and feelings when teaching new content and skills. If you feel anxious or stressed, look for ways to work on those stress levels and try to connect them to what is creating this feeling: is this the new content you want to teach? Is this the curriculum? Is this related to specific students or parents? Talk it through with someone you trust or journal about it.

Seek feedback and support from trusted people

Avoid asking for feedback from negative people or those who you know make you feel worse. Rely on your tribe of peers. Reach out to those who studied with you to share your experiences of teaching new concepts in the classroom or tackling a new curriculum or syllabus content area. You may have a colleague in your school, or another, with whom you studied at university, who is teaching exactly that content and those skills. Share your knowledge.

 What can you do to support building your self-efficacy to ensure you are looking after your wellbeing as a teacher?

 **Let's reflect**

Reflecting upon yourself as a person

As well as supporting your students' learning, you will be engaged in your own ongoing learning as a teacher. You will become an accomplished lifelong learner, and you will develop, enhance and strengthen your tools of the trade as you grow in your teaching career. This will impact you as a person. You may learn something completely new that you didn't realise you had an affinity with. You will also develop stronger and even new metacognitive skills and you will be blessed with being exposed to many opportunities for professional development with your colleagues.

 How confident are you acquiring new skills, knowledge and content?

If you can reflect upon this, you will understand how your students may feel when encountering something new in the curriculum.

Teaching new things is not just about content, it also requires new skills.

 How do you go about learning new things? How do your students go about it?

Helping and supporting your students in thinking about their metacognitive skills will build their trust in you as their co-agent of learning.

Reflecting upon yourself as a professional

As you have embarked on your journey of lifelong learning, you will also obviously engage in teaching new things to young minds within classrooms. You can be an inspiration to your students by sharing that you are also learning new things after you have attended a professional development course or a conference. Do not underestimate the capacity of your students to appreciate your own learning, especially if your new knowledge makes it easier for them to understand a topic.

Teaching new things effectively and with satisfaction specifically relates to AITSL Professional Standards 2, 3 and 6:

- **Standard 2:** you know your content, and how to teach it – you learnt that at university – but you may also have background knowledge and skills from other studies and life experiences. Always focus on keeping it simple and trust what you have achieved so far.
- **Standard 3:** you plan for effective teaching and learning. Lesson planning is key. Your school will have guidance on this. Stick with the curriculum and diversify as required.
- **Standard 6:** obviously, curricula and syllabi change and evolve, and so does your teaching. Do not feel you are stuck in a certain way. Being flexible will help you and your students achieve success and create a community of practice.

Let's get practical

Think about how you can set up a supportive classroom environment where every student can experience success. When planning lessons, how can you create learning experiences where your students know you believe they can succeed? For example, how can you use cooperative learning strategies, hands-on activities and varied methods of instruction to engage students with the curriculum? How could you develop their metacognitive skills in regard to their learning?

Think about how you can differentiate goals for your students. How can the goals you set influence the learning experiences you create, relevant to your students' skills and knowledge?

Think about how you can personalise your teaching in an authentic way to ensure both you and your students enjoy the process.

Let's do something about it

Take the time to reflect on your self-efficacy both professionally and personally. Periodically identify areas where you would like to learn about something that is new to you or that you may need support with. Only you know best what assistance you need and when. Trust yourself and then seek assistance. What professional learning opportunities will further build your self-efficacy? Who could you reach out to for further discussion?

Final words

Teaching is a profession we choose for one main reason: our passion to make a difference in the lives of those we teach. Always remember that you have worked hard to develop the knowledge and skills you have now, and you are working even harder to further develop them throughout your career. As a teacher you are more than just an educator. You are an influencer, who is always under the microscope of the school community you belong to. It may feel that everyone is entitled to have an opinion about what you do and how you should teach, but not many have undergone the teaching journey you and your peers have. You can turn this to your advantage: you are a champion of continuous improvement, and what you do counts. Remember, positive thinking is critical to be able to equip your students with the tools they require to keep them exploring and discovering as they learn.

CHAPTER 5

I FEEL LIKE PEOPLE AT THIS SCHOOL CARE ABOUT ME

No society can long sustain itself unless its members have learned the sensitivities, motivations and skills involved in assisting and caring for other human beings.

– *Urie Bronfenbrenner*

Michael's story

Starting my very first teaching role during the pandemic certainly taught me how fragile life can be. It also bought to the forefront the stresses and workloads educators must manage, and showed me the importance of teachers and how we need to make sure they are cared for. I went from the excitement of setting up my classroom and planning the ways I was going to make learning fun and engaging to quickly having to adapt to new routines and safety protocols and learn new hybrid ways of teaching. My mental health and wellbeing were truly tested during this time. As a graduate teacher I was on the frontline: not only supporting my students, but also their families as they transitioned to hybrid/remote learning.

Many teachers in my school were experiencing the same challenges and feelings and our school leadership team recognised this. They were quick to establish support networks we could lean on and made it clear they were here to help us get through this tough time.

My school cared about its staff, students and parents equally. Our leadership team spent time supporting the whole school community through communication that helped all involved to accept the uncertainty we faced, and to understand what was achievable by teachers, parents and students in the current situation. This helped set realistic expectations and ease anxiety.

Our leadership team set up regular check-ins with us and were diligent in staying on top of our stress levels and concerns. They would often give us prompts that encouraged honesty regarding how we were feeling. I was provided with a dedicated mentor and peer-to-peer support, which focused on my mindset and my feelings about my pedagogical ability given the circumstances. They listened and worked through solutions with me.

One afternoon we received a quick survey from our principal where we had to describe some of our favourite sweet treats and hot beverages. During that week, we all received a gift and a note of gratitude.

Now, following the pandemic, I can confidently say the people in my school really care about me and continue to. I am provided with ongoing feedback during lesson planning, I am encouraged to seek opportunities for growth and most importantly I am inspired to love what I do.

Writing your story

Caring is essentially a foundation stone of being moral. Being cared for by your school community and demonstrating care in your school community is crucial, especially since we often deal with students, families and colleagues who may be vulnerable.

 Think about what makes you feel that people care for you, either within your school community or personal life.

Think about a time you felt stressed or challenged, either as a pre-service or graduate teacher. How did the people around you support you to manage this?

What experienced teachers say

Caring promotes a connected school community and strengthens collaboration and wellbeing for the entire school. Have a read of the stories below describing other teachers' experiences around caring.

 I remember how hard it was to be a graduate teacher. I wasn't given a mentor as a graduate – I had to do a little searching to find them. I knew I had found the right mentors for me by the way they responded to when I asked a question, by not getting knocked back

when I needed assistance and by the resources they shared with me. The one thing I learnt was not to expect everyone to care and support me just because I was a graduate. I had to find people who were willing. I was lucky to have found some mentors in my first few years who took the time to care for me and recognise I was a graduate. Now, as an experienced teacher, whenever I am given the opportunity to mentor a graduate, I take it very seriously. – Callum

I'll never forget the feeling of being exhausted in my first term as a graduate teacher. I was sleep deprived, my immune system was low, I remember having the sniffles all the time! Information kept being thrown at me. I couldn't think about three months down the line, I was focused on getting through each week. My teaching partner at the time could see that I was overwhelmed, and one afternoon during planning took the time to check in with me. We spoke about my concerns and how I was feeling. We discussed a plan, particularly around how they could support me with information flow. We put the plan into action and my teaching partner made the time to regularly check in with me to see how I was moving along with the plan and if I needed support to make any further adjustments. – Jo-anne

Finally having a classroom on my own, I quickly realised that setting up routines would make teacher life much easier. I had some ideas from what I had observed during placement, but never really had the opportunity to set up routines from the get-go. On placements, I had always followed the routines already in place. I dabbled with a few ideas but found that I needed a sounding board to talk them through. I was working in a school that had a great culture, and during lunch break, I sat *in the staffroom and started to talk to my colleagues about what I was doing. My colleagues were great at listening to me and letting me share my thoughts. Instead of telling me what I should be doing, they started to share with me what they do, and asked me questions that prompted me to analyse the things I do. No one dismissed me or made me feel silly with what I was expressing. I remember walking away that lunchtime feeling that my colleagues cared enough about me as a teacher to support me to find resolutions. – **Nadia***

What is caring in schools?

Caring in a school context extends further than caring about students, colleagues, parents, learning and teaching. It also encompasses the quality of relationships you form with the school community and with yourself – your professional identity. It is the substance, method and motivation of your actions and interactions with others. It is a core quality of the communities you cultivate in schools for both students and adults. It is a crucial element of the social networks of families and communities, where children learn and grow.

Caring aims to promote the improvement and success of you and others. It is driven by positive values such as compassion, empathy, kindness and respect. It also relies upon growth and reflective mindsets such as thoughtfulness and motivational orientation towards others' needs, concerns and interests. Caring in schools is also enabled by competency, as you apply the knowledge and skills that bring your classroom, as well as your pedagogies, to life with positive and authentic learning experiences.

Passing your sense of caring on

Caring for yourself and others builds connectedness in school communities. It allows for teachers, students and parents to form positive professional relationships, share resources, feel valued and grow trust.

You and your school

Caring isn't as straightforward as you are showing care so that others show it back. You cannot assume that caring is always present in your school. In saying this, many teachers care deeply about their students and colleagues, but at times can be stressed, tired, busy or do not have the support to express their care effectively. There is an assumption that caring is the same for everyone, but as discussed in previous chapters, we all come from different cultures and backgrounds and may have diverse views on what caring is.

It is important to recognise the challenges surrounding caring in schools may be symptomatic of broader social trends – for example, the breakdown of community, socio-economic needs, weakening of social connections and the rise of individualism to a social media society. Furthermore, approaches that governments have taken recently regarding curriculum and testing may have influenced schools and made it more difficult for the people within them to develop supportive communities.

That said, as a pre-service or graduate teacher in a new school, you can bring a fresh outlook on caring. Share resources and stories, volunteer for projects and committees or find someone you haven't had much interaction with and have a chat. Even under challenging circumstances, be present in the school. Carry out specific (or even random) acts of kindness and continue to get to know your students and colleagues. It will make a difference, helping to strengthen your school connections and foster a sense of care.

 Think about a school you have worked in. How did you and your colleagues engage and interact to build connectedness within the school community?

You and your students

Academic challenge and pressure without sufficient caring and support may lower academic outcomes and performance. An Australian research study in early childhood education and care looked at the quality of preschool education and the results of NAPLAN tests in Year 3 in the same cohort of children. Unsurprisingly, the research found that the quality of socio-emotional relationships established between children and their educators was the best predictor of academic success in the primary years (Thorpe et al., 2015). Emotional relationships trumped quality of instruction and classroom contexts, settings and resources. School outcomes, high expectations, rigour and teacher–student accountability are also important when it comes to student academic success – but equal attention needs to go to the care and support necessary for your learners to respond positively to the challenges and expectations placed upon them. You must work on your growth mindset to enable students' positive mindset as well (we'll talk more about this in Chapter 6).

The goal to provide the care and support necessary for students' school success and to be a facilitating agent of their wellbeing is an exciting one to nurture and contemplate. By doing so, you will get a lot of care and support in return.

 Think about how you can use your own strengths to improve your students' sense of feeling cared for.

You and your colleagues

It's important to remember that while some of your teacher colleagues may have more experience than you, they all went through what you are going through as a graduate. It is critical that you demonstrate care for them as professional colleagues and people even if your levels of experience differ. At times it may be as simple as active listening and asking them how it is *really* going. Nurturing caring relationships with your colleagues will improve your sense of belonging, which has been defined as individuals feeling 'accepted, appreciated, and understood' in relationships with others (Riley & White, 2016, p. 211).

This means listening to others' stories and showing interest; being trustworthy and reliable if they tell you something in confidence or ask for genuine assistance; and supporting your colleagues and paying it forward. If you have a special skill, let your colleagues know and offer to share your knowledge. Reverse mentoring – where a less-experienced person shares their knowledge with someone more experienced – is powerful.

Teaching can, at times, be a stressful job. Sometimes your colleagues will need their space. It is important to be able to read a room. If you see a teacher in a conversation with another colleague, or enjoying lunch by themselves, just keep moving. Don't bother them. Respecting your colleagues' boundaries is critical to building bridges and keeping the workplace civil. And if you borrow something, return it in a timely manner.

 What teacher skills or talents do you have that you could share with your colleagues to show you care?

You and parents

Building strong and reliable connections with parents is key to student success. It is not about becoming friends; it is about building caring relationships for everyone's benefit.

Let's think about this. Parents are children's first teachers, guiding them to acquire the basic skills they will use their whole lives – from eating and sleeping to talking and walking. Parents watch their children move from infancy to toddlerhood, from preschool to primary school and beyond. Most parents love their children with their whole hearts, and they are sharing their child with you for the greater part of the day. Some parents may be struggling. Most parents are doing the very best they can with what they have. Be compassionate. Remember that for some parents, school was a source of stress and anxiety, so even communicating with you, as the teacher, may be difficult even without their children involved. Caring means recognising that the parents' own perception of schools and teachers may be biased. Even being in the school building may be stressful or scary. Some parents may be intimidated by you, unsure of the curriculum and confused about how best to support their children. Many parents may not know the educational jargon you use, but may be afraid to ask for clarification. Speak kindly to parents without being condescending. Leave your 'teaching voice' in the classroom and use a different tone with adults than you may use when speaking to younger children. Provide resources for parents where they can find more information, and gently point them in the right direction when necessary. Help parents help you. Allow parents to volunteer in your classroom or send them home with objects to cut, organise or sort. Parents want to do their part to help, so let them. Most really do care – ultimately, parents are human and feel the same way you do. They have good days and bad days, just like their children and just like you. So if a parent doesn't sign a form right away or calls you the wrong name at some point, just breathe through it. If you connect with a parent on the phone or via email, consider starting the conversation by saying something nice about their child.

 Think about the diverse backgrounds of your students' parents that you have come across. How did you support them in being part of their child's learning journey?

The connection with wellbeing

Caring is critical to our mental, physical and emotional health. It underpins our success as teachers. If you think about it, what is the alternative to caring? Not caring, or uncaring? When you are stressed or scared, you may fall into the trap of not caring and become cynical about the teaching profession. You know that this is not beneficial, does not align with the AITSL Professional Standards and could also be counterproductive, as it will make you miserable in the long run.

There is a challenge ahead of you as a teacher in the 21st century. Society is suffering from a serious erosion of social connections, and mental health is at risk. The most recent statistics from the Australian Institute of Health and Welfare (2024) found that, since the COVID-19 pandemic, there has been a substantial deterioration in children's mental health starting from prolonged periods of lockdown. This has especially hit hard children with pre-existing conditions and families in financial distress (Renshaw & Seriamlu, 2021); although since 2020, the everyday lives of all children, families and communities have been significantly affected by the pandemic and its aftermath (Martin et al., 2024). Changes to the way we live, the way we learn and the way we work, and a lack of predictability to how we live our lives, bring inevitable stressors, concerns and threats to our health and wellbeing (Tucci et al., 2020). As recently reported by the Australian Childhood Foundation, the most critical causes of children's stress have been related to a combination of increased screen time and reliance on social media, parents' stress around family health and job security, and a deterioration in socialisation opportunities and skills (Australian Childhood Foundation, 2024). Family and social life have been impacted significantly, which validates that while caring for our students' socio-emotional wellbeing may be at times challenging, it's imperative in our teaching roles. Showing you care is crucial. Following are some ways you can show you care.

Respect your own and others' individualities

Check people's pronouns, and learn their preferred name and how to pronounce it correctly. Mastering difficult pronunciation and being interculturally aware is essential to being 21st century citizens and modelling best behaviour. Be mindful of cultural and family differences when talking about challenging subjects and festivities, for example Mother's and Father's Day. Also be careful about topics such as divorce and death.

Greet everyone with kindness

In the school grounds, in the classroom and when you see them out – do not avoid people in your school community! Everyone loves to be seen and considered. Do respect boundaries if they clearly pretend not to see you, though.

Show respect and celebrate wins

Ask your students to help write the class rules. Show you care by asking their opinions. Acknowledge the strengths of each student, parent and colleague. Share strengths in the staffroom when appropriate, to celebrate someone's talent and skill. Enthusiasm about a student, parent or colleague can be contagious and create a culture of celebration and positivity. You can celebrate in-school wins as well as those that occur out of school, such as charity participation, running a marathon or entering an art contest. Find one thing in common with someone you may have difficulty relating to, and have an ongoing conversation that's just for them. Make a connection that isn't schoolwork-related.

Notice what's happening

You're in a school to teach, but you can't help but observe who's estranged from their friend group and who's disengaged. Talk to them. While everything else might be falling apart, at least one person has noticed them.

Show up

Attend school events, fundraisers and other community activities. For many, a school is about much more than academic achievement alone. You can show you care by being present outside the classroom, cheering everyone on, letting them see you as a person as well as a teacher.

 # Let's reflect

Reflecting upon yourself as a person

Caring for yourself and others is a key part of being a teacher. It's also a community-building responsibility. Think of an opportunity you have had in your life to volunteer or do something that had a direct impact on someone in need. Reflect upon times when you have received support in moments of need.

 What helped you feel better and cared for when you were vulnerable?

How could you care for and respect yourself and others through your teaching?

Can you think about authentic ways to instil your and others' talents, passions, heritage, skills and individualities in your lesson planning?

Reflecting upon yourself as a professional

Demonstrating care for yourself and others is a significant factor in progressing from an early career teacher to the later, more accomplished, stages of your career. It's also deeply related to all the AITSL Professional Standards; however, let's focus on Standard 4: creating and maintaining supportive and safe learning environments; and Standard 5: assessing and providing feedback and reporting on student learning.

 How do you create learning contexts that facilitate subject matter know-how as well as promote reflective and metacognitive skills? How do you instil your and students' individualities to show that you care about who you and they are as individuals?

How can you report and assess while caring for both subject knowledge and skills, outcomes, and your students' wellbeing?

Let's get practical

Teacher life can get busy; however, it is important to make time to stay connected with your colleagues. Try pencilling in regular days and times to meet up with your teacher friends, online or in person. You can use this time to check in with each other, talk about successes and problems or simply just to laugh and not talk about work at all.

Practise being open and trusting. Sharing your thoughts and feelings can make you feel nervous and vulnerable. Remember, you are not alone in the teacher world. Some of your colleagues will have similar thoughts and feelings. Practising having honest and open discussions can support both you and your colleagues in having a safe space for these types of conversations.

Practise small acts of kindness. Be aware of how your colleagues might be feeling on a particular day. If you know someone is having a particularly tough day, make them a coffee or tea, or maybe relieve them five minutes early from yard duty. Looking after each other on those challenging days can help us all feel less alone.

 ## Let's do something about it

Your colleagues are one of your main sources of support in a school community, especially in your first years of teaching. Take the time to reflect on who you are as a colleague. How can you develop positive professional relationships to help you and your colleagues survive and thrive throughout your teaching career?

Final words

Developing and maintaining support systems within a school community is crucial to our mental health as teachers. Caring is a service that fosters a sense of belonging and connection and can build a foundation of success for all. If we were to ask you what you remember most about your favourite teacher, chances are you'll talk about how they made you feel. The same is probably true of your favourite placement or school you have worked in. Keep caring at the forefront of everything you do, and you will reap the rewards.

CHAPTER 6

I HAVE ACCOMPLISHED A LOT AS A TEACHER

Keep on beginning and failing. Each time you fail, start all over again, and you will grow stronger until you have accomplished a purpose – not the one you began with perhaps, but one you'll be glad to remember.

– *Anne Sullivan*

Rhonni's story

In one of my first experiences of needing to call a parent to ask for a meeting with them, I was a mix of emotions. I wanted to discuss their teen's increasingly disruptive behaviour and their being on track to failing the subject, due to lack of focus in class, falling behind on tasks and failing a recent assessment. The need to make this call was keeping me up at night, grappling with how to best approach it. Each passing day that I didn't make the call it felt all that much harder to do.

I rationalised that my delay in making the call was because I was strategising about how to tackle the conversation honestly, respectfully and constructively (which was true). However, a large factor in the delay (when I was being honest with myself) was that I was procrastinating – putting off the task, as it was a tough one. How would the parents react? Was it my lessons that weren't engaging their teen? Was I doing all I could in class to manage the behaviours?

After grappling with this on my own for quite a few nights, it dawned on me that perhaps discussing this issue with my colleagues would be a good idea. Surely they had dealt with this situation before and so could provide me with some ideas? Leaning into that support was one of the best things I could have done. My colleagues were so receptive and generous with their gems of experience, ideas and support. They normalised the way I was feeling, effectively said 'You'll get very used to this', and reminded me parents are humans whom, overwhelmingly in the majority, appreciate the early broaching of a teacher's concerns about their child's progress. They shared stories of their own experiences for when such a call had gone well (and when it hadn't gone so well), and brainstormed with me on how I could approach my call.

One key tip that I received in that conversation with my colleagues was from someone who'd been teaching for many (many) years. He told me about a Mark Twain expression I'd never heard – about 'eating a live frog first thing in the morning'. Essentially the idea is that eating a live frog is so bad, that once you get *that* out of the way, it's hard to imagine anything worse can happen to you in the day. It's about doing the most challenging task first thing. It helps you to concentrate on getting *that* task done, and you can focus your thinking while you're fresh. It gets the 'worst' thing for your working day in the 'done' basket before you do anything else. I took that advice and made the call before the first class the next morning.

The 'eat the frog' strategy not only got me through those early couple of challenging calls with parents, but it also became a central tenant to how I approached my teaching life. Over time, with a kind of 'feel the fear and do it anyway' courage and practise, I developed the habit to get *the one most challenging task* out of the way first thing in the morning. Doing so gave me a sense of accomplishment from the get-go for the day, and I could enjoy and be present for the rest of the day's happenings. The procrastinating on the tough stuff became more or less a thing of the past in both my professional and personal life. I can't recommend the following teaching routine enough: wake up, have your coffee/tea/run/meditation, 'eat the frog', enjoy breakfast and embrace the day ahead.

Writing your story

Part of feeling a sense of accomplishment as a teacher involves being able to prioritise tasks you may find challenging, set goals that support your growth, and, most importantly, be kind to yourself by celebrating even the smallest of wins. Being able to identify your accomplishments can help you track your professional development and growth. Articulating what your accomplishments are can lead to success and can benefit your overall wellbeing as a teacher.

 Think back to your placements or your graduate year of teaching. What were your biggest accomplishments? How have these achievements helped you evolve in the next step in your career?

Name one thing you want to accomplish this year as a pre-service or graduate teacher. What steps will you need to take to make this happen?

What experienced teachers say

Experiencing a sense of accomplishment can be deeply fulfilling and rewarding. It involves not only navigating challenges and achieving goals but also having a positive impact on yourself as a person and professional. Have a read of what experienced teachers have said about accomplishment.

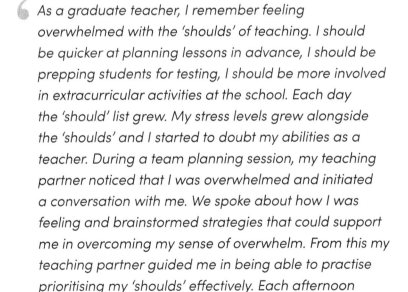

As a graduate teacher, I remember feeling overwhelmed with the 'shoulds' of teaching. I should be quicker at planning lessons in advance, I should be prepping students for testing, I should be more involved in extracurricular activities at the school. Each day the 'should' list grew. My stress levels grew alongside the 'shoulds' and I started to doubt my abilities as a teacher. During a team planning session, my teaching partner noticed that I was overwhelmed and initiated a conversation with me. We spoke about how I was feeling and brainstormed strategies that could support me in overcoming my sense of overwhelm. From this my teaching partner guided me in being able to practise prioritising my 'shoulds' effectively. Each afternoon before leaving for home, I would prioritise the most

important tasks for the next day; in the morning I would complete these first to support my progress towards feeling a sense of accomplishment. – **Fatima**

During my teaching placements, I found my direction and purpose in the classroom and with my students was mainly set by my mentors. As a graduate, I learnt very quickly that I needed to be able to identify and set these myself. During my studies I had read copious amounts of literature around goal-setting and had many opportunities to practise it. I made it a part of my routine as a gradate teacher where I would set weekly goals that I could accomplish. I would prioritise the tasks I thought would support me in making progress with either my students or as part of my teacher development, and I'd break them down into manageable milestones. One of the first goals I set myself was to continue to work on my time management in preparing my lessons. I set goals around specific times it should take me to complete certain tasks and practised using this to support me in ensuring that I used my given planning time at school to prepare as much as I could within work hours. – **Trung**

It was my first World Teachers' Day as a graduate. The cupcakes had arrived in the staffroom and a few of my students had arrived at school with flowers, chocolates and cards. I was feeling proud to be a teacher along with a great sense of accomplishment. But before I know it, the week had passed and the next one came around. World Teachers' Day had come and gone and that sense of accomplishment seemed to feel a little distant. In the staffroom, I often had causal chats with my colleagues about this. I remember one of my colleagues saying to me, 'As teachers, we naturally acknowledge *and celebrate our students' accomplishments each day, so why can't we do this with ourselves as well?' They were right. I needed to start to celebrate the wins no matter how small. I started to recognise each win I had and celebrated by either treating myself by buying something, or ensuring I took a self-care break by binge watching something or going for a spa day. Sure, World Teachers' Day was great, but we are teachers every day. Acknowledging the smallest of accomplishments helps you stay motivated and positive. – **Steph***

What does it mean to feel accomplished?

In Chapter 2 we have explored the concept of success. In this chapter we will explore the feeling of accomplishment as a teacher. You may be thinking, 'What is the difference?' Although success and accomplishment are closely related, accomplishments are the small, brilliant moments that underpin success. Think about an iceberg. Success is what you see, accomplishments are the foundations that you may not be able to see unless you reflect on them. This chapter will support you to recognise and celebrate your wins so that you can build a sustainable, successful career. Like pieces of a puzzle, it is critical you find, recognise, acknowledge and celebrate these moments as you build your career and become an effective teacher. Some of these moments will be expected as you will have worked on them; others will be the surprise effect of something that you have done, or emerge as a positive outcome of a challenging situation. Make time to celebrate your accomplishments, no matter how small.

In Australia, World Teachers' Day is celebrated every year in October, but you must take the opportunity to stop, reflect and celebrate your accomplishments, and those of your colleagues, more often than once a year to make your career sustainable and enjoyable. In this chapter we will work through those tangible and observable experiences that help slowly create and develop the image of the teacher you want to be.

Passing your sense of accomplishment on

You may have heard the saying 'stop and smell the roses'. Well, this can also be true of accomplishments. Along the way you will get feedback and encouragement which will give you a sense of your teaching accomplishments. However, at some point it will be important for you to create that sense of accomplishment yourself, and remind yourself to enjoy the journey you are on.

You and your school

Everyone wants schools to do a better job of educating children – and when this is accomplished, it is cause for celebration. By recognising and celebrating your daily wins, not only do you contribute to your career development and professional vision, but you also contribute to a positive school culture. Celebrating wins leads to feelings of connectedness with the school ecosystem. According to Di Malta et al. (2022), feelings of connectedness help to mediate the relationship between professional and academic performance and wellbeing, or lack thereof. Students and teachers who are less satisfied with their performance and are over-critical about it can be less likely to celebrate small moments of accomplishment, which can then contribute to feelings of disconnection and loneliness within a school community.

 What is a tangible teaching achievement that you could celebrate right now?

You and your students

Achievements are the small steps that ensure your students get good grades and are satisfied with their progression and school life. Accomplishment is a way of feeling, being and supporting your students to recognise their own progress in learning and mastering a subject or skill. This is when they will feel a sense of fulfilment. For this to happen you need to move the emphasis away from academic achievement alone. Student accomplishment requires clearly defined objectives, goals and expectations with a realistic timeframe to complete work, a strong understanding of the fundamentals needed to complete tasks, and a 'reward'. It requires you to encourage students to keep going and show resilience in the face of challenges. Studies have shown that feeling a sense of accomplishment is an important element in students developing positive wellbeing over time, and a growth mindset (Yaeger & Dweck, 2020). Showing students how excited and proud you are to see them reaching their goals, even when small, is important to their wellbeing.

Don't be afraid to put on some music or set up games to celebrate your students. Think about how you could put a positive twist on something children do not like to do – for example, reading time in class could be traded with reading time under the trees outside.

It is important that you also help students find their own ways to celebrate their small wins, and encourage them to share with family and friends. A strategy we have both used in our own classrooms is to create a Wow Wall. Encourage students to proudly put their work or thinking on display. If their 'wow' was completed via video or on an electronic device, the students would simply put up a note directing others where to find their work. Encourage classroom visitors to come in and check out the Wow Wall too.

 Think about setting up your own Wow Wall. How would you start it? What would it look like? How would you encourage students and parents to use the wall to celebrate the small wins?

You and your colleagues

You and your colleagues are connected in many ways regardless of how many years of experience you have. At some point, you will all experience similar highs and lows. Getting to know your fellow teachers and the important milestones or goals they have, and sharing your own, will support you in finding accomplishments to celebrate as well as how to celebrate them.

In previous chapters you reflected on taking the time to get to know your colleagues both professional and personally, and here is where it may come in handy. For example, to celebrate a colleague's accomplishment, you may want to give them a personalised gift that reflects their personality. Another way to celebrate each other's accomplishments as teachers is to contribute to a sense of camaraderie. Camaraderie can help us all feel valued and connected. Don't be afraid to organise an event that can bring you and your colleagues together, allowing you all to have little fun. It could be something as complex as a trivia night, or as simple as setting some time aside in a staff meeting for a show and tell. Earlier we spoke of creating a Wow Wall for your students. Why not try one in the staffroom with your colleagues? However, not all accomplishments need to be celebrated in an extravagant way – a simple private note or comment to a colleague will always warm a heart.

 Think of a time a colleague recognised one of your own small wins. What did they do or say?

You and parents

Communicating school accomplishments with parents and the wider community is an important step in establishing positive engagement. There are recognised links between the support schools receive from families and the local community, and the school's success (academic and otherwise), and students' and teachers' retention and achievement (Mishra et al., 2020).

There are parents and carers who will be willing to partake in celebrating school accomplishments, but it is important to remember that there will be cultural differences in how people celebrate. You will need to use your intercultural competence and get to know the parents, and then you will be able to celebrate in a respectful way. In this way, sharing high levels of care, positive attitudes, motivation and encouragement can have a positive influence on engagement outcomes. In any school community you are part of, there will be ways for you to connect with parents to support them and their children to understand the school community, and to build trust. Consistently sharing visible accomplishments is key – for the specific child, families as well as the class. For example, celebrating cultural diversity by recognising and celebrating the diverse backgrounds and cultures represented in the school community fosters inclusivity and mutual respect. Organising multicultural events or projects that showcase different traditions and perspectives can deepen connections among students, parents and teachers.

 Think about your memories as a student. What were the most effective ways your favourite educators celebrated accomplishments beyond marks and scores? What made these moments special? How could you replicate this in a way that is genuinely yours?

The connection with wellbeing

Rewarding efforts and recognising accomplishments is one way we can help develop a growth mindset (Dehaene, 2020). A growth mindset is a belief that intellectual abilities can be developed, as opposed to a fixed mindset where intellectual abilities are believed to be unchangeable (Yeager & Dweck, 2020). Creating an environment where the act of teaching and learning is celebrated, instead of focusing solely on the 'demonstration' of learning through marks and scores, will help students recognise their growing intellectual ability and develop a growth mindset. People with a growth mindset 'are more likely to thrive in the face of difficulty and continue to improve', with a stronger effect being observed in those who are at risk of poor outcomes (Yeager & Dweck, 2020, p. 1270).

Developing your own, colleagues' and students' growth mindsets through celebratory activities might contribute to improved outcomes, as well as supporting wellbeing and providing immediate motivation. It is key that you support celebration without judgement and that your focus is on celebrating the incremental process of developing ability, rather than validating existing competence (which is what is termed a fixed mindset). By doing so, you will support everyone's short- and long-term outcomes and motivation. Let's look at some ways to celebrate accomplishments and help others do so too.

Take mini breaks away from study and work

Whether it's a lunch break or a longer break, these moments away from study and work have a positive impact on your wellbeing and productivity. Breaks have been found to be important in recovering from stress and restoring energy and mental resources, which in turn can improve performance (Geurts et al., 2014). Putting yourself into 'rest mode' helps you to make sense of your experiences through consolidating memories, reflecting on the past and contemplating the future. Positive time out does not have to be long. Short stints of only a few minutes away from mental stimulation help support mental wellbeing and boost productivity, with relaxation or social activities being beneficial – such as reading a book or chatting with someone. Encourage your students to take time off their digital devices, too. Just a few minutes' silence to celebrate peace will help them appreciate their own space and connect with their body. This applies to adults, too. Get off your devices during your mini breaks.

Celebrate accomplishments meaningfully

There are so many ways to celebrate accomplishments. You can include visual cues in the classroom (e.g. photos from excursions and favourite activities, wins in sporting events and other competitions, a beautiful finished artefact). You can reflect on students' personal accomplishments (e.g. academic accomplishments, getting a part-time job, extracurricular activities) and make wins visible, giving students space to discuss what they're proud of in front of their peers. You can do the same for yourself by creating a bank of collectable memories in a journal or on an online platform. Never underestimate the value of telling a student or colleague directly that you've noticed their accomplishments. Words are powerful. Showing them that you see their efforts will help them feel a sense of pride in what they are doing.

Record and visualise achievements as you go

You might be over the idea of creating portfolios and collecting data having done so during your university studies; however, this is your chance to continue the practice in a way that is genuine to who you are and that serves your own career purposes. Collect evidence of your teaching excellence from multiple sources with different weights and validity. Collecting, tagging and organising evidence of your chosen teaching achievements is now more important than ever. Some potential sources you can use to evidence your teaching excellence include:

- feedback from students (notes from verbal comments, or written comments)
- feedback from parents and peers
- self-evaluations and reflections
- a summary of your contributions to teaching-related activities, such as unit lesson planning, curriculum design, activity

supervision, mentoring colleagues and teaching-related administrative activities

- artefacts from projects.

Create your own bank of memorable moments and refer to it when you feel that imposter syndrome is creeping up in, or when you know it is time to move on and find your next adventure. Moving on to a new opportunity is not 'failure'; it is growth and development of self-awareness as a teaching professional.

 # Let's reflect

Reflecting upon yourself as a person

Think back to when you decided to enrol in your university degree and become a teacher. It is important to reconnect to those experiences, expectations, feelings and thoughts to rediscover your purpose and reconnect with your dreams. The fact that you are reading this book suggests that you are an early career teacher, which means that you graduated (or are about to), which is an accomplishment. Give yourself a pat on the back. Remember to reflect upon the journey thus far.

 When you decided to enrol in your teaching degree, what did you want to accomplish in the short and long term? What were your goals and intentions as a person?

Have you taken the time to go down memory lane to when you started off this journey, and celebrate your progress? This is the time to do so.

Reflecting upon yourself as a professional

The AITSL Professional Standards that closely underpin the concept of feeling accomplished are Standards 4, 5 and 7. As a teacher, at various stages of experience, you work towards creating the most positive learning environments. You provide feedback on many levels regarding your students' academic progression, and you engage with your colleagues and community. You can have a strong impact on your students, colleagues and the teaching community, and they can have the same on you. What goes around, comes around. This may sound cliché, but it is true.

 How have you contributed to a positive learning environment in your school recently?

Do you have clear goals for yourself and your students this term?

Have you been realistic, and have you been taking some well-deserved time off to reboot and recharge?

Let's get practical

Respect your time. We can't say this enough. Teachers are hard workers. They get to school well before starting time and can often stay back well after end of day, even bringing work home for the weekend. Yes, as teachers it is almost unavoidable to put in those extra hours to get things done. However, it is crucial that you recognise that you cannot endlessly do this and that your best is good enough. It's important to make time for yourself, your family and friends, and step away from work.

Know you are making a difference, even if you feel you aren't. Even when you have been a teacher for more than two decades like we have, you won't always see the difference you are making straight away. It can take years to see the impact you have had on a student. Remember this: one day, maybe ten years down the track, a student will trigger a wonderful accomplishment for you.

Consider key times to celebrate. Some terms of a school year are busier or more stressful than others. Think about the whole-school occurrences that may happen within terms, for example report writing, exams and assessments. Consider the timing of these and plan to do something with your colleagues that can bring happiness and relaxation. Don't forget to consider times of the year when a morale boost might be needed – for example winter, when days can be challenging and full due to indoor lunchtimes in inclement weather.

Let's do something about it

The role of a teacher is one of the most important jobs in our society. Doing the best you can every single day is difficult, but important. As an early career teacher, think about three things that will be an accomplishment to support you in moving from graduate to proficient teacher.

Final words

Taking time to celebrate the small wins and being able to say you have accomplished 'a lot' requires seeing and recognising your achievements, keeping a record of them, rewarding yourself for them properly, and contributing to a culture of celebration for the whole teaching and learning ecosystem you belong to. If you do not stop to breathe and acknowledge these moments, they may be gone and forgotten in a second. This could leave you feeling hopeless and always chasing success. Recognising the wins, no matter how small, is important to overcome your fears, so that you can grow and shape your professional pathway as you need.

CHAPTER 7

I AM TREATED WITH RESPECT AT THIS SCHOOL

Education takes place in relationships.

– Loris Malaguzzi

David's story

I chose to begin my teaching journey 700 kilometres from my family and friends in a town with around 2400 residents. I was the only graduate in the entire school. Being the new teacher on the block, in a rural town where the community was tight-knit, was going to have its challenges. One of my biggest fears was not being respected in a school where everyone knew each other. Were parents going to want their child to have the most experienced teacher? Were students going to want the teacher they already knew and liked? Were my colleagues all friends already?

On one of my placements, my mentor teacher said to me, 'A good teacher is more than the skills they acquire; it's also about the person they seek to be.' I needed to find my own way to create an environment around me where parents, students, my colleagues and I treated each other with respect, courtesy and dignity, while being able to have open and honest conversations and exchange ideas. I kept this at front of mind with each day at school. I did some research of my own, and created a framework I could use as ground rules to support myself. I wrote my ground rules down and always had them on hand, especially in my first year – this helped make my expectations clear in my own mind. Part of my framework was to ensure I listened to others' points of view, knowing that there may be disagreement. I made a conscious effort to keep discussions on topic and not about people, as well as avoiding offensive language and sarcasm, and speaking in an acceptable tone. Most importantly I learned who my students, parents and colleagues were.

It isn't always easy earning respect and, sure, I made mistakes – but I learnt from them as well. The best thing I did was just kept at it.

I stayed consistent with my approach, reflecting and adjusting as needed, and in doing so I became a stronger professional and person. Oh, and I absolutely adore the community I am now part of, and can confidently say the feeling is mutual.

Writing your story

Respect is about showing appreciation, consideration and deferential regard to another person. It is the result of engaging openly and supportively with people from diverse backgrounds to create a positive culture. It is a vital part of establishing an environment where everyone knows they are valued.

 How do you show respect for yourself, others and the environment?

How have you experienced respect in your life? Think about your relationships with family, friends and colleagues, as well as environments in which you've felt respected.

What experienced teachers say

Being part of creating a culture of respect, and then working in that culture, will have a positive impact on you personally and professionally as well as strengthening the entire school ecosystem. When your students, parents and colleagues feel respected you are more likely to work effectively together, leading to less stress and conflict and improved collaboration and productivity. Let's hear what experienced teachers say about respect.

 As a graduate teacher I had a lot to learn, especially when it came to earning my students' respect. I knew this was something I had to do as quickly as possible to give myself the best chance of not ending up with difficult students. Firm but fair classroom management was my approach. On day one, after we spent the morning introducing ourselves and settling into our seats and lockers, I went

*straight into outlining the rules and expectations of the classroom. I needed to ensure that students were clear of these and understood the consequences, both positive and negative. I ensured that I enforced the rules and expectations. It did take time to work out how to get the right balance between being firm, but fair, but it was well worth the constant vigilance. Students in my class were never surprised by an outcome as expectations were clear and I always followed through. – **Kate***

I clearly remember my very first parent-teacher interviews. They were at the end of Term 2. I had been conscious of ensuring that I communicated with parents individually throughout the first half of the year when a student faced challenges or achieved successes, socially, emotionally or academically. I wanted to ensure parents were not completely surprised about their child's progress at a parent-teacher interview or when reading a mid-year report. I had this one student who acted up when they didn't get their own way in class. I had a conversation with their parent previously and thought we were making gains. I was ready to let the parents know of the success their child experienced and the areas we would be working on next. As soon as the child's parents sat down, before I could even say anything, the mum said, 'My daughter has always been the teacher's pet, so it's not fair that she isn't yours.' At that point everything I had prepared to say went out the window, and I was left a little shocked. I composed myself, as I knew I needed to remain calm, accept the situation and not retaliate. The interviews only went for 15 minutes, so I knew I was not going to be able to address the issue fully. I let the parents speak and showed them that I was concerned for their child and how together we could focus on their needs. I suggested *setting up another meeting to talk about it more. In fact, we had a few follow-up meetings, and slowly but surely we resolved the situation with the parents even reflecting back on their comment at the interviews and having a little giggle together. – **Sam***

*When I started my first teaching position one of my worries was stepping on my experienced colleagues' toes. I was conscious of building lasting, respectful professional relationships. As a graduate I was lucky to have been assigned a mentor, who gave me guidance in this area. The first thing they told me was that the quickest way to damage any teacher relationships was gossiping and spilling secrets. When someone tells you something in confidence, keep it to yourself. When you hear gossip, don't participate. Demonstrating that you can be trustworthy is a fundamental step in gaining respect. – **Karen***

What is respect in schools?

Creating a culture of respect begins with the internal capacity of teachers and students to be respectful towards themselves and others. Nurturing this internal capacity involves fulfilling the fundamental social and emotional needs required for a sense of belonging and a sense of self. Tending to students' social and emotional needs is a critical task for teachers, and essential in creating a culture of respect. This is facilitated through the caring relationships you have with your students.

A powerful component of the implicit curriculum is the 'beingness' of teachers. We teach who we are, whether we intend to or not. The way in which we interact with students, colleagues, supervisors and parents conveys messages, including about the level of respect we have for them.

Respectful schools are learning environments where every stake-holder feels safe, supported, engaged, nurtured and positively challenged. Respect doesn't happen in isolation: it is based on and thrives in relationships. Everything that you have discussed, shared and reflected upon so far now needs to be put altogether to consider the critical field of respect.

In a respectful school community, as members learn, teach and work together, they all seek to be respectful within the diverse social, emotional, civic and intellectual interactions that occur. Respect in schools means that absolutely everyone related to the school – teachers, parents, students, leaders and support workers, as well as those in the communities surrounding the school – are engaged and valued. Everyone must work together to develop and contribute to a shared school vision of respect. As educators, we should model and nurture approaches that highlight the benefits and value of learning. Ultimately, respect in a school is present when each person within the school's community contributes not just to the people, the learning and teaching processes, and the business administration, but demon-strates care for the school's physical environment and its values.

Passing your sense of respect on

A culture of respect allows for ideation, job satisfaction, efficiency and effectiveness in the school environment. When this occurs, staff are less stressed and more committed to their work. Let's take a look at how you can contribute to a respectful school culture.

You and your school

As an early career teacher, you may often feel as if society only recognises *some* things as important in schools – such as students' success in reading, maths and science, or NAPLAN results. Sometimes you may feel schools are respected only if they produce great results or put up amazing creative outputs for public display. You may feel your professional value is only related to tangible results. As important as results are, they do not alone recognise and consider the diverse voices of students, parents and teachers. Focusing solely on results, scores or public recognition may be one of the reasons children, teachers and parents alike feel disrespected and unheard. Beware of participating in and contributing to contexts that only value quantitative results.

A respectful school climate is one that values the learning process holistically – not just the logical, intellectual side of things, but also the social, emotional and community aspects. As an early career teacher, seek and contribute to schools that promote values such as freedom, social justice, common good, equality, diversity and honesty, as well as compassion and understanding. Emotions are contagious. When you feel listened to, taken seriously, appreciated and respected, you tend to 'pay it forward'.

A democratic school context has fairness at its core and focuses on ways for all students and adults to feel supported, despite the challenges that arise from achieving these goals (Cohen et al., 2008, 2010; Marzano et al., 2001). You can contribute to respect within your school by advocating for fair and equitable rules, and by involving all stakeholders in creating and upholding these.

 What examples can you think of where you may need to put your own or someone else's wellbeing before your duties related to assessments and teaching content?

You and your students

One common reason students often act disrespectfully is that they feel disrespected themselves – or they may need some modelling of what respect means. Even in the early years of your career, take the time to reflect upon the extent to which your students feel supported. There are several factors that can create barriers that undermine learning, and these often emerge from unmet needs. When a student is struggling with an undiagnosed learning disability or enters a new school for the second or third time in a year, they may need extra understanding and support. Ask yourself about the family situation your students come from. Respect may be as simple as changing the language you use so that you consider the diversity represented in your classroom. For example, consider using terms such as 'mum' and 'dad' carefully, as you may have children in your classroom who are raised by grandparents or foster parents, or whose parents are separated or same sex. To be respectful, it is critical that you consider the range and diversity of situations in your class and that you use proper language to make them feel included: consider their families, communities, habits, customs and histories. It may not always be possible to know every single detail of a student's life, but you can still make a concerted effort to avoid exclusion through your language.

Try to meet your students' unmet needs (which are different in every school and for every student) and you will become a champion of respect in your school. Respect with students is also about having fair rules for all. A good way to democratically create rules for the class is to involve students in creating a list of fair rules, which align with the school values and expectations, but also incorporate students' feedback. If you tell students they are not following 'your' rules, they may well think (or say), 'Well, these rules are your rules, not ours!' Again, respect is contagious: show respect and you will get it back.

 Can you think back to times during your university studies when you felt mostly respected and when you did not? Can you explain what the difference was between the two occasions? What lessons can you draw for your own classrooms?

You and your colleagues

Your teaching peers, at times, may also need support and encouragement. As adults, we are supposed to be stronger than our students and better able to manage our feelings and emotions, and also have the power to choose working environments that suit our needs, but let's be honest: all of us struggle with this at times. We all need respect and acknowledgement that we are ongoing learners, too. Some schools sadly do not recognise or support teachers' needs, which can inadvertently contribute to teachers feeling isolated and disrespected. As a colleague, and especially filled with the enthusiasm of your early career (along with some jitters), you can contribute to building a community that allows teachers to share their vulnerabilities with colleagues. Be there for your colleagues and respect their uncertainties during tough times. Keep any private disclosures confidential and share when it is important to share, and with the right people who can help. Step up; don't hide behind the 'early career teacher' label. You have a lot to contribute when you're fresh out of university.

Also be aware that, as you reach out to mentors and coaches, you may not always agree with the strategies, ideas or methodologies they share with you. Regardless, respect others' contributions and be thankful for their willingness to share. We all have reasons behind our actions and decision-making. As a graduate you don't need to apply or follow every piece of advice you receive, but you can certainly be grateful and contribute to a culture of sharing. What would schools look like if all teachers could share best practices in a trusting, nonjudgmental forum?

As a new teacher to a school, you can also help to dispel myths about senior teachers (e.g. Mr Smith is strict and never shares, Mrs Smith is always grumpy). Do not contribute to stereotypes or share gossip. To promote safe schools and model this behaviour to students, we must support the entire school community to stand up for others. In a respectful school, people notice and respond in socially responsible ways to cruel, mean, unjust and bullying behaviour. Do not be a bystander if you witness colleagues being belittled.

 Can you think of a time you showed respect for someone's point of view even though you didn't agree with it? How did you go about it?

You and parents

Like any relationship, that between parent and teacher will benefit from timely and early established positive interactions. As we discussed previously, parents are their children's first teachers. While they may at times sound overly opinionated to you, most have their children's best interests at heart. They are not against you, they are pro their children. Effective, ongoing communication based on mutual respect will usually flow if you establish these channels nice and early.

As the University of Queensland's Dr Linda Willis, an expert in parent engagement, says: 'First impressions are really important. I think if parents or teachers are seen to be unapproachable it doesn't allow the relationship to develop on a good footing' (QIS Parents Network, 2023). Take the time to create quality school–family relationships and have the students' best outcomes in mind. Ultimately, parent engagement is critical to successful learning. This starts from early childhood and continues through to high school. When carers are involved and the communication starts early, students do better academically, stay in school, are engaged in their homework, behave better, have better social skills, are more motivated to learn and go on to successful post-school pathways. It is key that you see parents as partners in the teaching and learning business. Tricky situations are always going to happen every now and then, but if you already have mutually respectful relationships with families the outcome will be more positive.

When parents express concerns about their child in relation to something that happened at school, ensure you plan a time to talk to them when you are in a good position to be open-minded, clear, calm and free from stress (for instance, avoid straight after a last-period class on a Friday). Negotiate a time that suits both parties, suggesting times when you know you will not be overloaded yourself.

Finally, remember that some students may not have supportive parents or may have very difficult situations at home. As a teacher, sometimes you are one of the few adult carers who can be there for the student. Respect these students and their backgrounds and do not judge. Reach out to experts who can help when needed, and stand up to be the adult carer who takes an interest in these children's lives.

 How can you help bring what the child is learning at school and what the parent knows about what their child is learning at school closer together?

The connection with wellbeing

Respect has a lot to do with wellbeing at both the personal and professional levels. It relates to having a positive feeling of appreciation for someone (be that a colleague, parent, leader or student) and also to the specific actions and behaviours that represent that appreciation. Respect can be defined as allowing yourself and others to do and be their best. This starts with yourself: appreciate who you are, look after yourself and nurture your identity and values. You will then be able to do the same for those around you, in life and at school.

Respect will also support the sustainable progression of your career, as you decide on your pathway and vary your direction to ensure you always find yourself in nurturing environments and contribute to those, too. Respect breathes life into relationships, supports resilience through adversity and promotes equity. It is the foundation that allows for problems to be overcome. Respect does not make a school 'perfect', but it does make a school an effective, nurturing environment that people want to be part of. This creates a strength-based and growth-focused mindset within the community.

Let's take a look at how we can nurture respect to support everyone's wellbeing.

Introduce democratic decision-making

Open dialogue engages students in a democratic process in which compromise rather than competition is the basis for decision-making. How about involving your students in how they would like their classroom to look? One idea is to rearrange desks for a day and see how that goes. This can work wonders as a circuit-breaker if students are distracted or something in your planning is not working. You could even move all the desks to the side and have students sit on the floor in a circle or in groups. Let students have a say; give them a chance to learn from their decisions. Democratic decision-making can become a great teachable moment regarding preferences, agreements and negotiations, and how these are all based on respectful interactions and relationships.

Use multidimensional classwork

Respect that your students all have different learning preferences. While it may not always be possible to cater to all tastes and modes, allow flexibility as to how students learn. Rather than forcing 'all eyes on you' there may be times when they could walk around the class, have earphones on with music or scribble while you are talking. If you set democratic class rules, you can draw on these in case things get out of control. If things do go pear-shaped, this can be a teachable moment around the balance between personal freedom and others' rights.

Vary how work is presented

Sharing in and about classrooms often comes through talking or writing. It is important to respect your students' many skills and talents by using, for instance, visual representations of learning without using language. Brainstorm with your colleagues or students around the diverse 'identities' that emerge in school – the writer, the thinker, the talker, the visual artist, the technology guru and so forth – and how these might be accommodated in the classroom.

 Let's reflect

Reflecting upon yourself as a person

As an early career teacher, you may at times have self-doubt, feel exhausted when you try new things, continuously ask for reassurance or feel overwhelmed when you receive feedback. Take time to care for yourself, as we discussed in Chapter 1. This is the first step in respecting yourself. Practise what you preach, have clear boundaries, and always pick the right times to challenge yourself and try new things when you are ready for it.

 What are some practical strategies that you can put in place to ensure your 'time off' is respected by your colleagues, parents and students?

Reflecting upon yourself as a professional

Each domain of the AITSL Professional Standards is underpinned by respect, especially in the Professional Engagement domain, in particular, Standards 6 and 7: 'Teachers demonstrate respect and professionalism in all their interactions with students, colleagues, parents/carers, and the community. They are sensitive to the needs of parents/carers and can communicate effectively with them about their children's learning' (AITSL, n.d. a). The Professional Standards describe the need to engage in professional learning, which allows you to show appreciation for yourself as a teacher and to professionally engage with colleagues, parents and the community. As we have discussed, you are an important carer in students' lives, so always ensure that you nurture your sense of respect so you can model it and pass it on.

What are some practical ways to model self-respect and self-care in your classrooms?

What types of professional learning could you seek that focus on wellbeing?

Let's get practical

The way in which you interact with your colleagues, students and parents will form the basis of how they see and respect you. In all your interactions, be yourself and be honest. Work on creating genuine relationships by keeping it real. Take time to show appreciation, listen attentively, and find ways to bring out the best in people – whether they are an adult or child. Showing you are invested in the people who make up the school community will earn you respect.

Asking questions and seeking guidance from your colleagues is an effective way to build professional relationships and respect. It's also a great way to show your colleagues that you value and respect their experience. Nobody wants to see you fail – they would much rather be part of your success.

As the saying goes, to earn respect, you need to show respect. By showing respect to your students, you are also modelling the behaviour you expect from them. When students feel they are being treated with respect they are more likely to treat each other (and you) the same way. Showing respect to your students can also lead to them feeling valued and understood, and this can be just the motivation they need to work harder and enjoy their learning journey.

Let's do something about it

When reflecting upon respect, related concepts such as honesty, gratitude and appreciating differences emerge strongly. Showing respect in the classroom and staffroom is not always an easy task, but when we start reflecting on these concepts, we can see the steps we can take to improve respectfulness all around us – among our peers, parents, leaders and students. A practical way can be starting off with a gratitude journal: find one thing each day you are grateful for, and at the end of the week, write a note to one person to show you respect their actions, ideas, initiative or just a simple gesture they did that you noted down. Encourage your students to do the same in the classroom with a gratitude wall or gratitude jar, and reflect on how explicitly expressing appreciation for others' actions, gestures or ways of being is a way of showing respect towards that person.

Final words

To genuinely feel that you are respected as a teacher, your teaching colleagues and the whole school community must feel respected too. As an educator who is key to supporting young people's holistic growth, it is important that you look after yourself, and that you constantly work on respecting your and others' bodies, minds and spirits. You must strive to show compassion for and understanding of the differences you will most certainly encounter, and reflect upon when it is time to stay silent and when it is time to speak up. Through daily practice, you can make this frame of mind contagious in the classroom and staffroom.

Remember that you are not alone in this teaching journey. Engage with your leaders, peers and school community, practise compassion and tolerance, and you will set upon a sustainable and empowering career path of genuine growth. There is no harm in trying, nobody's perfect, and being a respected teacher is a journey, not a destination.

CHAPTER 8

I FEEL LIKE MY TEACHING IS EFFECTIVE AND HELPFUL

How can we, with our adult minds, know what will be interesting? If you follow the child ... you can find out something new.

– *Jean Piaget*

Louise's story

Throughout my teaching degree and into my early years of teaching, I was always involved in discussions around the qualities of a good teacher. I became proficient in rambling these off: patience, empathy, communication, adaptability, just to name a few. I always reflected on how I was using these to ensure I was helping my students learn new things. But the real reflection came 12 years later.

In my first year of teaching I taught prep, then in my second year I followed the same group of students to Grade 1 as their teacher. I formed great bonds with these students and their parents over these two years. I got married the year I had Grade 1 and I clearly remember the joy I felt when students and their parents came to the ceremony in support. I did lots of cooking with this group of students as part of their learning and had a team of wonderful parent helpers on rotation. On school holidays, I would even send home holiday packs, just in case any students needed ideas.

Fast forward 12 years and a change in schools. One day a student from my previous prep/Grade 1 cohort presented themselves at my classroom door, with a pen from Swarovski and a thank-you note. They had just completed their final year of secondary school and wanted to thank me for all I did in their junior years in helping to give them a start. This student went as far as calling schools in the area to locate me, as I had moved on. I could not believe that, all these years on, the impact I had remained in their mind. In their note they thanked me for being fair, humorous, creative and caring, and it was at that moment that I truly understood that I was good at helping students learn new things. Those were the effective qualities I used most.

As teachers, we work tirelessly to educate and guide the students in our class. So, remember, you might not always see the impact of your work immediately, but teachers change students' lives every day. And when that moment of realisation comes, it's incredible.

Writing your story

Effective teachers make a difference in the lives of their students, colleagues, parents and school community. It is often these teachers that students think of or come back to thank years later. As a teacher you will have a long-lasting influence on the students you teach. You will directly impact how and what your students learn as well as the ways they interact with each other and the world around them.

 What educators in your schooling life were helpful to you on your learning journey?

Think about what type of teacher you want to be. What words would you like to use to describe yourself? What could you do to gauge whether you are meeting your own expectations?

What experienced teachers say

Being a helpful and effective teacher extends beyond content expertise. It incorporates understanding different ways to teach effectively, being prepared, having clear expectations and, most importantly, patience. As discussed in Chapter 7, you set the tone of the class with your example. If your students can feel your commitment to helping them learn, your teaching will be more effective. Giving your students a positive reason to remember you as their teacher is a rewarding part of your teaching journey.

Let's see what some experienced teachers say about effective and helpful teaching.

My journey as a teacher began in 2010 in a secondary school setting. I quickly realised that the students in my very first class were faced with a range of challenges, from learning difficulties to troubled parents. I also had a handful of students who were disengaged from learning and appeared to lack a sense of purpose. I knew that I needed to create a classroom that would foster a sense of community and trust for learning to occur. In talking to my colleagues, I learned that one of the strategies they used was the power of storytelling. I began to use this strategy in my teaching to help my students see connections between their own lived experiences and those of others. Slowly but surely, I began to see changes, from behaviour to engagement to confidence. This was reassuring and showed me that my teaching was helpful and effective. – *Tilly*

'Overwhelming' is the word that first comes to me when I think about my first year of teaching. I spent my time planning, differentiating curriculum and analysing data. Even though this was all important, I felt I wasn't spending time making connections with my students. To work out what some of colleagues were doing I made time to chat to them. I also tried to observe the way other teachers communicated with students, on the playground and at assemblies and school events. I noticed one teacher was shooting hoops with students every Wednesday for half of lunch. Another would eat their lunch with their students once a week as a class picnic. I even noticed one teacher making the effort after school to pick out a few parents to let them know of something great their child did at school that day. I started to see that that these teachers in their everyday interactions with students were constantly building their *relationships. I wanted to be that teacher, too. I made some small changes to make my relationships with students a focus. I started with something that I could easily maintain; I called it the 'morning meeting'. We started each morning gathered as a class in a circle. I got students involved in doing different class greetings and then we played a game or had a chat. I used this time to give an outline of the day as well. This small shift stated to change the feeling in the classroom. I was happier at school, and so were my students. – **Ellie***

*I remember sitting in a workshop and the question was asked, 'If your students were asked to describe you, what words would you hope they use?' I wrote down four words: encouraging, fair, passionate and fun. I took these words back to my classroom with me and kept them where I could see them. I made them my mantra for my first year of teaching, reflecting on how I demonstrated these things in my class and with my students. Towards the end of each term, I would do an activity with my class, asking them to write down words that best described each other including myself. It was rewarding to see that students used words such as fun, fair, kind and helpful. – **Tim***

What is effective and helpful teaching?

Throughout each chapter, we have built a vision of what it means to be a teacher: a professional educator who has a positive impact on students, the school community and themselves and is grounded, satisfied and content with what they do. An effective and helpful teacher's profile encompasses all the skills, knowledge, strengths and challenges we have discussed so far, underpinned by professional and personal reflective work that aims to strengthen resilience while acknowledging vulnerability.

There are many ways to teach effectively; we are all different educators with different stories. Nevertheless, good teachers share many common qualities. They are prepared, set clear expectations, have a positive attitude (or try hard to keep one), are patient (and have good buddies to help them keep this way), and do not only assess students, but also their teaching on a regular basis. These teachers are helpful because they genuinely care for their classrooms and take time to get to know their students and their families. They understand that education is about much more than the transmission of knowledge, and they're committed to creating the ideal conditions for learning, for real understanding, for every child in their class, every day.

Passing your effectiveness and helpfulness on

To make a lasting impact on your students, you need to use effective teaching practices. By doing so, you pass on not just knowledge but a sense of empowerment, curiosity and resilience, leaving an imprint on your students' lives.

You and your school

Graduate teachers have so much to contribute to their schools. You bring fresh ideas about the curriculum, having only recently applied critical pedagogical approaches while on placement and learnt new ones, too. Do not underestimate the contribution you can bring to the whole school community. Every graduate teacher will be different. You may also have specific key learning area expertise. Bring all your knowledge thus far with you and share new, innovative ways to teach. Of course, you will seek guidance and advice from leaders and senior teachers, who will provide mentoring and coaching; however, don't be afraid to practise and share what you already know.

 What is something you have tried in your classroom or on placement for the first time? How did it go?

You and your students

The idea of being helpful and effective for every single child in your classroom may be intimidating – by now, you know a classroom is made of students with diverse personalities, stories, family backgrounds, cultural systems and needs. As an early career teacher, you need to start asking yourself how you can help students (from a very early age) to identify by themselves what they need and want to discuss, rather than working this out for them all the time. It is a matter of power used well, because you have the ability, as the professional educator, to direct or influence your students' self-discovery.

In the classroom, teachers exercise 'power' in the materials and resources they select, the learning activities they design, and how they include students in tasks and discussions. Knowing this, it is important to think about how you can consciously use this power for good, shift the power dynamics in the classroom, and empower your students to be agents of their learning. If you only focus on your students' challenges, this may undermine their sense of self and their ability to engage in class. We recommend you use a strength-based approach that helps them identify their strengths, talents and interests. A focus on students' skills celebrates resilience and resourcefulness, and creates growth mindsets. Fostering genuine care for students means holding high positive expectations for all of them, and believing in their potential for growth. Numerous studies suggest that when adults have high expectations for students, students feel more motivated and achieve more. Encourage a context where your students can learn to take the reins in monitoring and reflecting on their learning through portfolios, one-on-one conferences and peer sharing.

Remember: everyone has a little bias. It is critical to acknowledge any possible biases you possess and ensure that your care is genuine for every student. You must hold the same positive expectations for all of them, and communicate belief in everyone's potential for growth. Your expectations may be the most powerful force in the classroom.

Have you ever experienced a situation when you felt someone had a bias towards you? How would you go about reflecting on your personal biases and overcome them?

You and your colleagues

Biases are for everyone, so also reflect on any biases you may have regarding your colleagues. To be helpful and effective as a teacher-colleague and to contribute to your community, it is critical that you hold those high expectations for every one of your colleagues, no matter how old they are, how senior, how young, how more or less experienced than you, what university they attended, what accents they have and so forth. We are not perfect, and we will hold likes and dislikes in regards to some personalities. We are not meant to be 'everyone's friends' in the staffroom, but it is important to contribute to a positive, respectful, professional as well as compassionate staffroom – schools are truly and uniquely an ecosystem, where someone's failure can affect everyone. Equally important is not overdoing it. You may be tempted to be overly helpful to all senior staff to make an impression or because you feel you owe them. You know your worth and you are a teacher among teachers: so to be able to be helpful to others and effective in a classroom environment, it is also important to find and trust your voice and speak up when you need to. Schools often need fresh voices and fresh outlooks.

 Can you remember a time when you were very helpful to someone whom you really admired (be that family, friends, a teacher or an academic at university)? How did that make you feel?

You and parents

To be genuinely helpful and effective as a teacher, focusing on how you communicate with parents and how you make them feel is critical. Vary your communication style according to what works best for each family, within boundaries. We know one size does not fit all, and genuine equity is giving others what they need. For example, think about whether all your parents have access to email. Provide some options that you are comfortable with to support communication. Follow-through is just as important: if you promise something, you must deliver it.

You do not have to respond to emails or phone calls after hours or on weekends. Parents will understand that you have a life outside of school. If you read an email or text out of hours that requires a quick response, send a short reply that you'll investigate it as soon as school is back.

Parents appreciate hearing the good and the bad when it comes to how their child is going. Let them know that you're taking their child on a learning journey, with all the triumphs and failures that go along with it. It is important to be friendly but professional, and use lay terms when talking about the curriculum. There is no need to overwhelm them with pedagogical jargon to demonstrate you are a good teacher.

It is important to remember to not take things personally. If parents complain about something, do your best to make them feel heard and understood. If necessary, bring in the principal or your leader as a mediator. And if you made a mistake, show the parents that you are professional enough to acknowledge this. Parents will not lose respect for you if you show that you are wanting to take their feedback on board and improve your professional practice. As all educators know, you never stop learning.

 Can you remember a time when you were very helpful to someone whom you really admired (be that family, friends, a teacher or an academic at university)? How did that make you feel?

The connection with wellbeing

The foundation for effective and helpful teaching and successful learning is underpinned by the promotion of wellbeing in the whole school community. A school has processes and policies in place to ensure a healthy sense of belonging and positive relationships to support students, teachers, parents and helpers to feel safe and respected, while also encouraging everyone to be the best version of themselves. You as a teacher play a leading role in supporting (or, at times, creating) such a culture. You cannot do it alone, but you can and must contribute to it. This is a big part of what makes teaching an exciting job.

For this to happen, you have to look inward first and seek your own wellbeing, so that you can thrive and extend into being as helpful as you can be. Your teacher wellbeing relates to healthy habits, resilience and self-efficacy, social-emotional competence, personal responses to your students and colleagues' work, and acknowledging and addressing signs of burnout, fatigue, exhaustion and stress. Being effective requires us to work on our relationships with the meaningful 'others' at school (and, by now, you know there are a few). Focus on being mindful and reflective, particularly when it comes to work-life balance. Seeking support from professional learning communities so you can contribute to creating a positive school ecology.

Here are some strategies to increase your and others' wellbeing through effective and helpful teaching.

Prioritise relationships

Effective and helpful teachers prioritise building relationships – with students, parents, colleagues and leaders. They make authentic efforts to get to know the people in the community, especially their students and their needs. Positive teacher–school relationships play an important role in student wellbeing. They form a foundation for effective teaching and learning. Sitting down for a frank chat with a colleague, student or parent may pay off more than any PD would.

Contribute to motivation and autonomy in the school community

Autonomous motivation is grounded in the widely accepted self-determination theory, which suggests that autonomously motivated students display increased persistence and enjoyment in their studies, perform better, are better able to deal with challenges and have reduced anxiety (Kearns, 2017). The same can be said for yourself, colleagues and leaders in your school. How could you support everyone's intrinsic motivation? Positive feedback and reinforcement are not just reserved for students. Everyone needs encouragement, principals included.

Keep calm and focused, and be kind

Help yourself and school stakeholders to slow down and reduce stress by engaging in brief periods of mindfulness, or any activity that makes people slow down: it may be a chat with students outside rather than in the classroom, a brisk walk with a colleague to discuss a challenging case, or a cup of tea in the library to plan a lesson with your mentor. Be the one with the initiative to create a circuit-breaker in how you strategise for efficacy, and think differently how you engage with others. Also remember to practise active listening and seek others' thoughts and feelings. There is nothing like asking someone, 'How are you?', and truly listening to what they say, to make them (and yourself) feel instantly better.

Let's reflect

Reflecting upon yourself as a person

Being a helpful and effective teacher is a lifelong journey. As you grow you will go through various stages – just like the different stages of the AITSL Professional Standards, from graduate to highly accomplished (and, even then, the search for efficacy and helpfulness keeps going). Effective teaching encompasses many processes, practices, skills and knowledge sets, alongside your own story as a person and your journey as a teacher. It is everything that sits alongside achievements under the iceberg that we call success.

 What are the foundations that help you be and feel effective and helpful?

What motivates you in keeping on this path? (Nobody else can answer for you, except you, because the answer is different for all graduate teachers.)

Reflecting upon yourself as a professional

AITSL Professional Standards 3 and 4 epitomise the focus on helpfulness and effectiveness. To maintain a sustainable, long-lasting career, being able to seek and provide help and support will be a key feature of your progression. This will ensure stability, support good mental health, and will ultimately sustain a sense of belonging, which we discussed in Chapter 1 as a key factor. The Professional Standards focus on key concepts such as planning for, implementing, creating and maintaining effective and safe teaching and learning contexts. Think about the 'here and now' – your answers may change as you progress further in your teaching journey.

At this point in time, what do you think your biggest strength is when it comes to contributing to effective academic contexts?

What is something you want to work on and develop further?

 ## Let's get practical

Encouraging students to work on solutions in groups with peers they don't tend to socialise with is an effective way to teach a lesson and get your students working as a team. It is particularly useful in the upper year levels with students who like to choose the same group to work with each time.

Set clear standards and expectations that both you and your students follow. Your students need to know what is acceptable and what isn't. Have these visible in the classroom using a mixture of words and pictures.

Reflect, and then reflect some more. This is key to being an effective and helpful teacher. As a teacher your professional development is ongoing. Simply ask yourself what went well and what you would do differently next time. Not every lesson you teach will work out the way you planned, and that is okay. Reflect on it and learn from it.

 ## Let's do something about it

To be an effective and helpful teacher you need to be able to teach *all* your students. Your student cohort will be made up of people with various abilities, interests, cultures and values, along with varying degrees of confidence and curiosity. Make it part of your daily routine to find ways to get to know each student and build rapport. This will help you foster an inclusive approach to teaching and learning, prompting students to participate in class with increased motivation.

Final words

Being a positive influencer as a teacher should be one of your goals. Making students feel safe and worthy can make a difference not only to their learning, but to their life. You never truly know what students may have encountered before becoming a part of your class, or what conditions they go home to. The same can be said of your colleagues, leaders and whomever you meet in the school community you are a part of. Each day is a new day, and a new opportunity to try something original and learn something different. So don't forget to smile, be patient and be kind to others, starting with yourself.

Conclusion

We hope this book supports you in making connections between your own teacher journey and those of your colleagues. We wrote the book we wish we had been gifted when we were early career teachers, and hope it will be a trusted companion for your first few years out.

We want to encourage you to prioritise your wellbeing. This in turn will help foster a positive environment within the school ecosystem you're part of. In writing this book, we drew upon our extensive experience in the field of education with a focus on improving graduate teachers' wellbeing. We hope the book helps you, and your students, to be happier in the school environment. We wanted to highlight the importance of recognising your professional role as a teacher, as well as you as an individual distinct from your profession. Our hope is that this book improves the overall quality of the teaching profession.

Throughout history many experts, from teachers to philosophers and psychologists, have shared their insights, research and findings. We can draw upon this wisdom in different ways and for different purposes throughout our teaching lives. The quotes we chose for this book are from those who have inspired us during our teaching careers. We realised that, when we were studying to become teachers, we didn't fully appreciate or understand the ideas we read about – until we started teaching and put theory into practice.

As you develop and experience your professional journey, all the theoretical learning you were exposed to will come back to you. You'll connect the theory with your daily practice. This is when you'll start building deeper connections to the Professional Standards allowing you to transition from graduate to proficient teacher.

Throughout your career you will find other experts whose insights will have an impact on you, big or small. These people may be from different fields – for example, conference speakers, colleagues, your local and school community, researchers and authors, just to name a few. Take the time to identify and acknowledge their contribution in your teaching and, where possible, connect with them, making them part of your network.

Your graduate years of teaching are exciting and challenging, filled with to-do lists that seem never-ending. It's racing to yard duty with a half-eaten banana in your hand, while wondering if you switched off the laminating machine. There will be tears, laughter and moments in which you're not sure whether to laugh or cry. You will go from feeling on top of things to wondering how other teachers make it look so easy. Recognising your stresses plays a critical role in understanding how to manage your responsibilities as a teacher. We encourage you to seek guidance and advice from teacher mentors and school leaders when you feel your wellbeing needs attention. Your colleagues want to help you be successful. Most importantly, working out a work-life balance that suits you is crucial. How you care for your own wellbeing will have a flow-on effect to the students and families who are part of your classroom, and the wider school community. Wellbeing is about taking care of yourself physically, mentally, emotionally and socially, and it is this type of self-care that will allow you to thrive and survive as a teacher in the 21st century.

Remember, go slowly and take the time you need to learn new things. Refuel your creative energy, develop connections with those who matter and remind yourself that teaching is a journey worth undertaking and persisting at. Keep yourself connected to why you became a teacher in the first place, and adopt a growth mindset. Create clear boundaries between home and school and establish good sleeping and eating habits. Reward yourself, be kind to yourself and allow yourself to always put your day into perspective.

Lastly, we hope while on your teaching journey you make some very good friends for life, just like we did.

About the authors

Celia is a qualified primary school teacher with a Master of Education in Student Wellbeing. She has over 25 years of teaching experience, both face-to-face and online, including mentoring pre-service and graduate teachers. Recently Celia has been involved in leading, managing and shaping the overall strategy, development, design and delivery of the professional experience aspect of several online ITE courses in the higher education sector. Drawing on her communication, interpersonal, organisational and leaderships skills, Celia cultivates supportive learning environments guided by policies and frameworks, standards and goals.

Marghi holds 30 years' combined experience in the primary, secondary and university sectors. A qualified school teacher, published author and academic educator, Marghi also worked as an educational publisher and an ACARA curriculum writer. Marghi started her journey in online higher education in 2015 and, since then, she has become extremely passionate about hybrid ITE programs – they allow a wide range of diverse students, many from disadvantaged backgrounds, to follow their passion and become teachers. She currently leads the hybrid delivery of a Master of Teaching (Primary), which includes in-school placements. Marghi still teaches in a range of ITE degrees, both online and on campus, which allows her to actively mentor pre-service teachers through their academic and placement journeys. Marghi defines herself as a 'passionate lifelong learner' and she is currently a PhD candidate at Griffith University.

References

Ainsworth, S., & Oldfield, J. (2019). Quantifying teacher resilience: Context matters. *Teaching and Teacher Education, 82*, 117–128.

Allen, K. A., Slaten, C. D., Arslan, G., Roffey, S., Craig, H., & Vella-Brodrick, D. A. (2021). School belonging: The importance of student and teacher relationships. In *The Palgrave handbook of positive education* (pp. 525–550). Cham: Springer International Publishing.

Australian Childhood Foundation. (2024). *The impact of Covid-19 revealed.* https://www.childhood.org.au/covid-impact-welfare-children-parents/

Australian Institute for Teaching and School Leadership (AITSL). (n.d. a). *Australian Professional Standards for Teachers.* https://www.aitsl.edu.au/standards

Australian Institute for Teaching and School Leadership (AITSL). (n.d. b). *Australian Teacher Performance and Development Framework.* https://www.aitsl.edu.au/tools-resources/resource/australian-teacher-performance-and-development-framework

Australian Institute for Teaching and School Leadership (AITSL). (n.d. c). *Domains of teaching.* https://www.aitsl.edu.au/standards/understand-the-teacher-standards/domains-of-teaching

Australian Institute for Teaching and School Leadership (AITSL). (2022). *Wellbeing in Australian schools.* https://www.aitsl.edu.au/research/spotlights/wellbeing-in-australian-schools

Australian Institute of Health and Welfare (AIHW). (16 April 2024). *The health of children.* https://www.aihw.gov.au/reports/children-youth/health-of-children

Australian Institute of Health and Welfare (AIHW). (2018). *Mental health services—in brief 2018.* Cat. no. HSE 211. Canberra: AIHW.

Australian Institute of Health and Welfare (AIHW). (2019). *Australian Burden of Disease Study: impact and causes of illness and death in Australia 2015.* Australian Burden of Disease series no. 19. Cat. no. BOD 22. Canberra: AIHW.

Bandura, A. (1997). Behavior theory and the models of man (1974). In *Meeting of the American Psychological Association,* Aug, 1974, New Orleans, LA, US; Presidential Address presented at the aforementioned meeting. American Psychological Association.

Barbeau, L., & Cornejo Happel, C. (2023). *Critical Teaching Behaviors: Defining, Documenting, and Discussing Good Teaching.* Stylus Publishing.

Bates, T. (2019). *Teaching in a Digital Age.* Simon Fraser University.

Bronfenbrenner, U. (1979). *The ecology of human development: Experiments by nature and design.* Harvard University Press.

Brookfield, S. (2010). Critical reflection as an adult learning process. *Handbook of reflection and reflective inquiry: Mapping a way of knowing for professional reflective inquiry,* 215–236.

Cohen, J., Pickeral, T., & Levine, P. (2010). The foundation for democracy: Social, emotional, ethical, cognitive skills, and dispositions in K–12 schools. *Inter-American Journal of Education for Democracy, 3*(1), 74–97.

Cohen, J., Pickeral, T., & McCloskey, M. (2008). The challenge of assessing school climate. *Educational Leadership, 66*(4).

Commonwealth of Australia. (2014). *Teacher quality: evidence review.* https://www.dfat.gov.au/sites/default/files/evidence-review-teacher-quality.pdf

Dabbs, L., & Howard, N. R. (2015). *Standing in the gap: Empowering new teachers through connected resources.* Corwin Press.

Dehaene, S. (2020). *How We Learn.* Penguin Books Ltd.

Di Malta, G., Bond, J., Conroy, D., Smith, K., & Moller, N. (2022). Distance education students' mental health, connectedness and academic performance during COVID-19: A mixed-methods study. *Distance Education, 43*(1), 97–118.

Fenstermacher, G. D., & Richardson, V. (2005). On making determinations of quality in teaching. *Teachers College Record, 107*(1), 186–213.

Flores, M. A. (2020). Feeling like a student but thinking like a teacher: A study of the development of professional identity in initial teacher education. *Journal of Education for Teaching, 46*(2), 145–158.

Geurts, S. A. E., Beckers, D. G. J., & Tucker, P. (2014). Recovery from demanding work hours. In M. C. W. Peeters, J. De Jonge, & T. W. Taris (Eds.), *An introduction to contemporary work psychology* (pp. 196–219). Wiley Blackwell.

Golzar, J. (2020). Teacher identity formation through classroom practices in the post-method era: A systematic review. *Cogent education, 7*(1), 1853304.

Graham, L. J., Tancredi, H., & Gillett-Swan, J. (2022). What Makes an Excellent Teacher? Insights From Junior High School Students With a History of Disruptive Behavior. *Frontiers in Education, 7*.

Hattie, J. (2011). *Visible learning for teachers*. Routledge.

Hewlin, P. F. (2020). How to be more authentic at work. *Greater Good Magazine.* https://greatergood.berkeley.edu/article/item/how_to_be_more_authentic_at_work

Johnson, Z. D., & LaBelle, S. (2017). An examination of teacher authenticity in the college classroom. *Communication Education, 66*(4), 423–439.

Kaider, F., Hains-Wesson, R., & Young, K. (2017). Practical Typology of Authentic Work-Integrated Learning Activities and Assessments. *Asia-Pacific Journal of Cooperative Education, 18*(2), 153–165.

Kaplan, J. S. (2000, July). A journey home: Teaching towards self-understanding. In Exploring myths and legends of teacher education. Proceedings of the Third International Conference of the Self-Study of Teacher Education Practices. Herstmonceux Castle, East Sussex, England (pp. 126-130).

Kearns, T. (2017). *Applying self-determination theory (SDT) in an emancipatory study with anxious adolescents to investigate any changes in anxiety and wellbeing* (Doctoral dissertation, University of East London).

Kreber, C. (2010). Academics' teacher identities, authenticity, and pedagogy. *Studies in Higher Education, 35*(2), 171–194.

Kreber, C., Klampfleitner, M., McCune, V., Bayne, S., & Knottenble, M. (2007). What do you mean by 'authentic'? A comparative review of the literature on conceptions of authenticity in teaching. *Adult Education Quarterly, 58*(1), 22–44.

Lee, M., Seashore Louis, K., & Anderson, S. (2012). Local education authorities and student learning: The effects of policies and practices. *School Effectiveness and School Improvement, 23*(2), 133–158.

Lemon, N. (Ed.). (2021). *Healthy relationships in higher education: Promoting wellbeing across academia.* Routledge.

Lemon, N. (Ed.). (2022). *Creative expression and wellbeing in higher education: making and movement as mindful moments of self-care.* Taylor & Francis.

Lemon, N. S., & McDonough, S. (2020). *Building and sustaining a teaching career: Strategies for professional experience, wellbeing and mindful practice.* Cambridge University Press.

Lemon, N., Harju-Luukkainen, H., & Garvis, S. (2022). Learning with and from One Another: Valuing Self-care as a Part of the Higher-Degree Research Student and Supervisor Relationship. In *Supporting Student and Faculty Wellbeing in Graduate Education* (pp. 176–189). Routledge.

Martin, L. N., Giff, S. T., Ribeiro, S., Fyffe, S., & Renshaw, K. D. (2024). Changes in relationship quality in the COVID-19 pandemic: associations with pandemic stressors and couple communication. *The American Journal of Family Therapy, 52*(2), 176–92.

Marzano, R. J., Pickering, D. J., & Pollack, J. E. (2001). *Classroom instruction that works: Research-based strategies for increasing student achievement.* Alexandria, VA: ASCD.

Minor, C. (2018). *We Got This. Equity, Access, and the Quest to Be Who Our Students Need Us to Be.* Heinemann: Portsmouth, NH.

Mishra, L., Gupta, T., & Shree, A. (2020). Online teaching-learning in higher education during lockdown period of COVID-19 pandemic. *International journal of educational research open, 1*, 100012.

NSW Department of Education. (n.d.). *Success stories.* https://education.nsw.gov.au/teaching-and-learning/aec/premier-s-priorities/success-stories

Nygaard, M. A., Ormiston, H. E., Renshaw, T. L., Carlock, K., & Komer, J. (2024). School mental health care coordination practices: A mixed methods study. *Children and Youth Services Review, 157*, 107426.

Nygaard, M. A., Ormiston, H. E., Renshaw, T. L., Carlock, K., & Komer, J. (2024). School mental health care coordination practices: A mixed methods study. *Children and Youth Services Review, 157*, 107426.

Organisation for Economic Cooperation and Development (OECD). (2011). *Building a high-quality teaching profession: lessons from around the world background report for the International Summit on the Teaching Profession*. Paris, France: OECD Publishing. http://fulltextreports.com/2011/03/16/building-a-high-quality-teaching-profession-lessons-fromaround-the-world

Organisation for Economic Cooperation and Development (OECD). (2021). *Education at a Glance 2021: OECD Indicators*. OECD Publishing: Paris.

Perkins, K. (2015). *Parents and teachers working together*. https://www.acer.org/au/discover/article/parents-and-teachers-working-together

Queensland Independent School (QIS) Parents Network. (January 16, 2023). *First impressions are important': Why forming a good relationship with your child's teacher is worth your time*. https://parentsnetwork.qld.edu.au/2023/01/16/first-impressions-are-important-why-forming-a-good-relationship-with-your-childs-teacher-is-worth-your-time/

Queensland Independent School (QIS) Parents Network. (September 19, 2019). Respect and courtesy: a healthy relationship with your child's teacher can help you negotiate tricky moments when they arise. https://parentsnetwork.qld.edu.au/2019/09/09/respect-and-courtesy-a-healthy-relationship-with-your-childs-teacher-can-help-you-negotiate-tricky-moments-when-they-arise/

Renshaw, L. and Seriamlu, S. (2021). *Australian Children and Young People's Knowledge Acceleration Hub – Sector adaptation and innovation shaped by COVID-19 and the latest evidence on COVID-19 and its impacts on children and young people Sep/Oct 2021 Digest*. ARACY and UNICEF (United Nations International Children's Emergency Fund) Australia.

Renshaw, T. (2022). *Teacher Subjective Wellbeing Questionnaire (TSWQ): Measure and User Guide*. https://osf.io/6548v

Renshaw, T. L., Long, A. C., and Cook, C. R. (2015). Assessing teachers' positive psychological functioning at work: Development and validation of the Teacher Subjective Wellbeing Questionnaire. *School Psychology Quarterly, 30*(2), 289.

Riley, T., & White, V. (2016). Developing a Sense of Belonging Through Engagement with Like-Minded Peers: A Matter of Equity. *NZ J Educ Stud, 51*, 211–225.

Russel, D. (2019). Value and authenticity in teaching. *Teacher.* https://www.teachermagazine.com/au_en/articles/value-and-authenticity-in-teaching

Shah, M. (2012). The importance and benefits of teacher collegiality in schools–A literature review. *Procedia-Social and Behavioral Sciences, 46*, 1242–1246.

Sianoja, M., Kinnunen, U., Bloom, J. D., Korpela, K., & Geurts, S. A. E. (2016). Recovery during lunch breaks: Testing long-term relations with energy levels at work.

Steele, A. R., & Leming, T. (2022). Exploring student teachers' development of intercultural understanding in teacher education practice. *Journal of Peace Education, 19*(1), 47–66.

Thornton, B., Zunino, B., & Beattie, J. (2020). Moving the dial: Improving teacher efficacy to promote instructional change. *Education, 140*(4), 171–180.

Thorpe, K., Cockshaw, W., & Edmed, S. (2015). The association of observed quality of early years classrooms (ECEC-Year 2) and NAPLAN outcomes: a study of E4Kids children in Queensland, 2010-2014. Department of Education.

Tucci, J., Mitchell, J. and Thomas, L. (August 2020). A Lasting Legacy – The Impact of COVID-19 on children and parents. Australian Childhood Foundation, Melbourne.

University of New South Wales (UNSW). (2019). *Teacher-student relationships crucial to student engagement.* https://www.unsw.edu.au/newsroom/news/2019/08/teacher-student-relationships-crucial-to-student-engagement

Von Münchhausen S., Braeunig M., Pfeifer R., Göritz A. S., Bauer J., Lahmann C., et al. (2021). Teacher self-efficacy and mental health—their intricate relation to professional resources and attitudes in an established manual-based psychological group program. *Frontiers in Psychiatry, 12.*

Xiyun, S., Fathi, J., Shirbagi, N., & Mohammaddokht, F. (2022). A Structural Model of Teacher Self-Efficacy, Emotion Regulation, and Psychological Wellbeing Among English Teachers. *Frontiers in Psychology, 13.*

Yeager, D. S., & Dweck, C. S. (2020). What can be learned from growth mindset controversies?. *The American psychologist, 75*(9), 1269–1284.

Zukav, G. (1999). *The seat of the soul.* New York, Simon & Schuster.